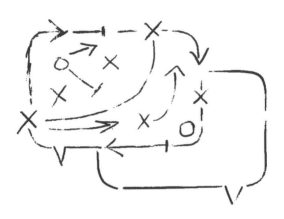

RETHINK
COMMUNICATION

*A Playbook to Clarify and Communicate
Everything in Your Church*

PHIL BOWDLE

ISBN: 9781792064562

Published by the Center for Church Communication
Los Angeles, California
www.CFCCLabs.org
Copyright © 2019 Center for Church Communication
Cover design by Joe Cavazos.

CONTENTS

Foreword   9

Introduction   13

New Reality   23
Attendance   27
Engagement   35
Attention   45

The Message and the Megaphone   55
The Ministry of Communication   59

Communication Playbook   67
Clarify Your Message   75
Craft Your Elevator Pitch   107
Brainstorm Creative Ideas   117
Develop Your Communication Plan   129
Execute Your Plan   165
Evaluate Your Results   173

Rethink + Rework   181

Mall Kiosks   185

Urgent vs. Important   191

A Simple Solution to Message Overload   195

Less Is More   201

Quit Doing Announcements   205

7 Reasons Why You're Not Getting a Stage Announcement   211

Social Media Playbook   215

7-Day Social Media Playbook for Pastors   223

You've Got One Job   229

Redefining Excellence   235

4 Questions Every Great Story Answers   239

Reaching Younger Generations   245

Healthy and Sustainable   251

A Last Word   255

Endnotes   258

Free Resources   259

About the Author   260

About the Center for Church Communication   261

More Church Communication Help   263

Acknowledgments   264

FOREWORD

BY TONY MORGAN

———

If you play a role in leading the church, God has placed you in a defining moment. A moment of tremendous change and tremendous opportunity.

I've been working with and serving the local church for more than 20 years. I've been a part of small churches, served on senior leadership teams at large churches, and now serve hundreds of churches through The Unstuck Group.

In all my years of working with churches, there are some consistent areas where churches find themselves stuck. Stuck in the areas like church growth, spiritual formation, giving, leadership development, and engagement. However, there's one area that too often gets overlooked. It's an area that has been an issue for almost every church I've seen or worked with. It also happens to be a root issue that holds churches back from addressing the most common issues facing the church.

That area is communication.

Here we are, living through the biggest communication shift in 500 years. The problem is, most churches are operating from the old playbook.

The old playbook for communication in the church was built around the idea that people would come to you. When they came, you'd have a chance to share your message with them through announcements, bulletins, and signs. As our culture has changed, we're seeing people attend church less frequently and communicate with a whole new set of rules. If you want to reach people with your message now, you'll need an intentional strategy for how to communicate when people are inside (physically) and outside (digitally) the walls of your church.

If the church is going to make the most of this defining moment, it's going to require something from every leader in the church. It's going to require the church to rethink communication. This book by my friend Phil Bowdle will help you do just that.

Rethink Communication isn't your typical church book. This isn't a book of rules to follow. It's a playbook to disrupt the way you've always done it. It's a roadmap to navigate through the changing world of communication. It's a call for everyone who shares the message of Jesus to rethink how we can effectively communicate in a way that cuts through the noise.

I've had a chance to work with Phil and see him lead through change. He has a knack for finding clarity in the midst of chaos and providing a system to help you do the same.

To navigate through the biggest communication shift in 500 years, you'll need a playbook. Here it is.

Tony Morgan
Founder and Lead Strategist at The Unstuck Group

INTRODUCTION

THE CHURCH DOES NOT HAVE A MESSAGE PROBLEM.

THE CHURCH HAS A MESSAGE DELIVERY PROBLEM.

I've got good news and bad news.

The good news?
The message of the gospel has not changed.

The bad news?
If you want to reach more people with your message, engage your congregation in the mission of the church, and grow your church by reaching the unreached around you—then it's going to require you to rethink the role, strategy, and ministry of communication in the church.

Whether you're a senior pastor, ministry leader, or communication leader in the church, you have a role to play, because everything communicates. Everything.

Every sermon.
Every event.
Every announcement.
Every sign.
Every handout.
Every website.
Every bulletin.
Every social media post.

Everything communicates.

Communication is something your church does every single week that literally impacts every person in your church.

Do you want to communicate your event, program, ministry, or initiative? Do you want someone to sign up? Show up? Give? Serve? Share? Accept Jesus as their Savior? It's going to take effective communication to help them take action.

How we handle communication has the potential to make or break your ability to reach and engage more people with your message. The words you use, way things look, timing, tone, and strategy all play a crucial role in whether your message is heard or ignored.

The Communication Problem Plaguing the Church

You'd think with all the new communication methods we have (such as websites, social media, video, email, texting, and beyond) that it would be easier than ever to communicate your message, right? Unfortunately, that couldn't be further from the truth.

Our message isn't the problem. Our delivery of that message is the problem.

It's never been easier to communicate a message. However, it's never been harder for that message to connect.

We're currently living through the most radical shift in how our culture communicates since the printing press changed the world. The digital revolution has changed everything.

It's not just the methods we're communicating with that have changed—it's the people and culture that have changed.

Churches everywhere are realizing the communication playbook of 30 years ago no longer works. What worked before isn't working anymore, and something needs to change.

There are new rules to play by, and it's time for us to rethink communication in the church.

The Greatest Opportunity

In Matthew 28:19, Jesus calls all of us to "**Go** into all the world and **proclaim** the gospel to the whole creation."

We as the church have a life-changing message with life-changing opportunities to communicate. Here's the great news: God has given us new opportunities to go and proclaim that message!

There's no doubt that all these changes with our culture and communication can be overwhelming. But there's nothing to be afraid of here. In fact, it's quite the opposite.

What if these changes spark some of the greatest opportunities we've ever had in communicating the gospel?

Never before have we had the opportunity to reach people all over the world at the click of a button. Never before have we had so many new tools and methods to engage people with our message of Jesus.

You are no longer bound to the one hour a week when you can communicate in person with those who attend your worship services. You now have the opportunity to reach and engage people during the other 167 hours of the week outside the church worship service.

This is a time to dream. This is a time to innovate. This is a time to rethink communication in the church, so we can take hold of these amazing opportunities to go and proclaim the gospel.

What will you do with these new opportunities?

How to Read This Book

There are many great books that speak to crafting the "macro" message of your church. This book will certainly help you do that, but it's not the sole focus.

What I want to do with *Rethink Communication* is give you a practical playbook to help you share all the "micro" messages in your church. You know… the things we do in the church every single week?

I'll get super practical about what it will take to communicate your message with clarity and remove barriers keeping people from taking a next step. Along the way, I'll share what you need to know about the new reality for what attendance, engagement, and attention look like for the church and the people you communicate with.

Before we go any further, here are a few things you need to know.

This Isn't Just for the Big Church or the Little Church

The principles in this book work, regardless of the size of your church, staff, or budget.

Don't Read This Book Alone

Communication isn't someone's job. It's everyone's job.

Communication can't just be outsourced to one person or one department. Every staff member and leader in the church has a role to play because everything communicates.

This is a book designed to be wrestled with as a team. So before you get too far, grab someone you do ministry with and work through this book together. Powerful things can happen if you can get leaders in your church to work together on becoming more effective in everything you're communicating.

One Last Warning

If I'm doing my job right, there are going to be things that motivate you, frustrate you, equip you, and challenge the "that's how we've always done it" mentality.

You won't agree with everything I say, and that's OK. That's not my goal.

My prayer is that this book will spark conversation for your church and give you a playbook to take advantage of the greatest communication opportunity in generations to put Jesus on display in your community, country, and world.

My Challenge to You

Communication has been overlooked for far too long in the church. It's time for that to change. That change starts with you. That change starts now.

Through the mighty power of God, everything you communicate can change lives and change someone's eternity.

Change is never easy.
But for what's at stake, it's worth it.

The church doesn't have a message problem.
The church has a message delivery problem.

Let's fix it.

NEW
REALITY

What changed with attendance,
engagement, and attention
in the church.

I grew up in the church. Literally. My dad was the senior pastor and my mom was the children's director, so I found myself inside the walls of the church a lot growing up.

Every Sunday, you could find me causing trouble for whoever was lucky enough to have the hyperactive pastor's kid for Sunday school class. Then, you could find me in the front pew of the church, making goofy faces at my dad while he preached.

Growing up, I was frequently asked, "Are you going to be a pastor like your dad?" Before they could finish the question, I would quickly say, "No!"

Well, here I am, all these years later, serving as a creative arts pastor, more fired up than ever before to see people's lives transformed through Jesus. God has quite the sense of humor.

Since those early days sitting in the front pew, it's been fascinating to see how the landscape of the church has changed.

The basic foundation of most churches has not changed dramatically. The average church is built around worship services, children's ministry, student ministry, Sunday school or small groups, and ministry events.

So what's changed? Well, it's more than just musical styles, discipleship models, and buildings. It's the people. It's our culture. The digital revolution and our changing culture are redefining how people are engaging with the church.

How do these changes impact the way we approach communication in the church?

The average church hasn't changed the way it communicates in the last 30 years.

The problem is the average person the church is trying to reach has changed.

Of course, many of the communication methods we're using now look different than they did 30 years ago. However, the way most churches approach communicating with their congregation and community is based on a foundation of assumptions that were made 30 years ago. Those assumptions can no longer be made. There's a new reality for effective communication.

I was speaking recently with a pastor in his 50s, and he was sharing how overwhelming the landscape of the church is today. He said: "I learned how to do ministry in seminary more than 20 years ago and what the generation before me taught me to do. What's challenging now is the way I learned to run the church before gave no consideration to the digital revolution we're in right now. The digital world of Facebook, Instagram, and YouTube is foreign to me, and I don't know where to start or what needs to change."

To discover what needs to change to communicate effectively, you must first understand the new reality for what **attendance, engagement, and attention** look like for the people we communicate with.

1
ATTENDANCE

WHAT WOULD NEED TO CHANGE IF YOU KNEW YOU ONLY HAD EIGHT TO 10 TIMES A YEAR TO COMMUNICATE IN PERSON WITH EACH INDIVIDUAL IN YOUR CHURCH?

Since the beginning of my time at West Ridge Church, where I serve as the creative arts pastor, we've been tracking a few key metrics. One of the many things we track each week is attendance.

Here's how those numbers have changed over the last eight years:

In 2010, the average person attended church every two to three weeks. In 2018, the average person attended church every five to six weeks.

That means for the average person in our church, we only have around eight to 10 times a year to communicate with them in person.

However, those numbers don't tell the whole story.

While the frequency of attendance has declined, each of these areas have grown:

- Average weekly attendance
- Membership
- Small group involvement
- Digital engagement
- Live stream views
- Giving

It's possible your church could be growing in the number of members, while at the same time your average weekly attendance is declining.

The new reality is that people are attending church very differently, and less frequently, than they did 30 years ago.

Recent studies from Barna[1] have addressed these changes:

> "From technology to politics, a lot has changed in 30 years. Spiritual routines are no exception. Church attendance, though still a vital part of many Americans' lives, has been inconsistent since Barna began tracking it in 1986. Back then, nearly half (48%) reported going to a church service in the past week. That number has declined and climbed over the years but has recently trended toward its lowest point yet (35%)."

What Is Leading to These Changes in Attendance Patterns?

Sunday Is No Longer Sacred

In many communities, it was assumed you were going to church somewhere on Sunday. That's an assumption we can no longer make.

Sunday morning used to be exclusively reserved for church services. Businesses would often close and activities would not be scheduled on Sunday morning. But today, Sunday doesn't look much different than any Monday through Saturday for most communities.

Busyness

The biggest thing keeping people from attending your church on Sunday isn't competition from other churches in your area, it's busyness. Sports, vacations, and recreation are crowding schedules, and it's impacting how often people choose to attend church.

Many of today's parents are in a situation their parents never faced. They have to choose between having their kids participate in sports or going to church. Sunday is no longer a sacred day of the week reserved for church attendance and family time.

The Growing Number of "Nones"

The sad reality for America is that there are an increasing number of people who have no religious affiliation at all.

The Public Religion Research Institute[2] indicates:

> "In 1991, only 6% of Americans identified their religious affiliation as 'none,' and that number had not moved much since the early 1970s. By the end of the 1990s, 14% of the public claimed no religious affiliation. The rate of religious change accelerated further during the late 2000s and early 2010s, reaching 20% by 2012. Today, one-quarter (25%) of Americans claim no formal religious identity, making this group the single largest 'religious group' in the U.S."

Generational Decline

Millennials (those born between 1981-2001) are connecting to the church very differently than other generations. Only 28% of millennials have attended church in the last week.

For gen-Xers (born between 1965-1980), 33% attended church in the last week.

In the book *Churchless*, George Barna and David Kinnaman speak to the changing attendance patterns by saying:

> "More Americans than ever are not attending church. Most of them did at some point and, for one reason or another, decided not to continue. This fact should motivate church leaders and attenders to examine how to make appropriate changes—not for the sake of enhancing attendance numbers but to address the lack of life transformation that would attract more people to remain an active part."

On-Demand Culture

The on-demand nature of our culture is disrupting "live" experiences everywhere. Take TV for example. More than ever before, TV shows are being viewed after they've aired live through DVRs and streaming services. People are still engaging with these shows, but they are doing it on their own terms, at their own preferred times.

Thirty years ago, if you wanted to experience teaching from your pastor, you needed to show up on Sunday at a certain time to hear it. Now, as technology has changed, there are limitless options to experience the same teaching without physically attending church through digital communication channels such as podcasts, live-stream services, videos, and more.

How Changing Attendance Patterns Impact Your Communication

To effectively communicate your message, you'll need to stop building your strategy exclusively around physical attendance. Why? As my friend Dave Adamson says, "Church attendance is not decreasing, it's decentralizing."

Thirty years ago, you could assume that if you shared an announcement two weeks in a row, you would be speaking to the vast majority of your congregation. Today, you can't make that assumption.

The reality is, attendance is great and it makes in-person communication easier, but that's never really been the end goal for the church. I've never stumbled upon a church mission statement that says, "Our mission is to have the highest attendance in town."

Attendance is not our mission. Making disciples is our mission.

If attendance patterns are declining, along with opportunities to communicate with the congregation in-person, how can we engage people where they are? That's what we'll cover next.

Discuss

- What are you noticing about the attendance patterns in your congregation?

- How are these changes in attendance patterns impacting your communication?

- What would change for you and your church if you knew you only had eight to 10 times to communicate in person with each individual in your church?

2
ENGAGEMENT

THIRTY YEARS AGO,
THE CHURCH'S GREATEST
COMMUNICATION
OPPORTUNITIES WERE
INSIDE THE WALLS
OF THE CHURCH.

TODAY, THE GREATEST
COMMUNICATION
OPPORTUNITIES ARE
OUTSIDE THE CHURCH.

If you've been frustrated by trying to manage the chaos of church communication, let me take a moment to explain how it got so chaotic.

Think of it this way...

Before the Digital Revolution

The playbook for communication in the church used to be simple. Before the digital revolution, communication in the church was like a two-lane highway. This highway consisted of two main ways of engaging people with your message.

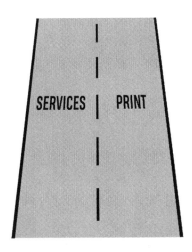

The strategy for communicating the messages of the church was usually confined by what you communicated in the worship services and what you distributed in print. This type of communication was dependent on communicating to people when they were inside the walls of your church. If you had something you wanted your church to know about and engage with, you could take time during the service to share those announcements or distribute a bulletin or handout full of information. This was one-way communication, from the church directly to the congregation.

These were simpler times in the world of church communication. At this point, the need for any dedicated communication staff was minimal because there were fewer lanes to manage. In fact, the "communication director" in most churches was the pastor or their administrative assistant.

After the Digital Revolution

After the digital revolution, communication in the church looks far more like a crowded, chaotic, seven-lane highway.

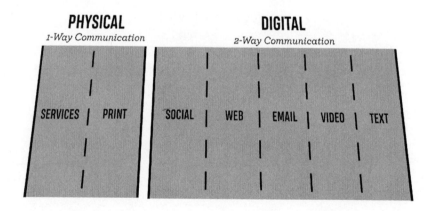

As people are attending church less frequently, and communicating through a growing number of digital communication channels, the playbook for communication is no longer simple. It's far more complex to get your message across when you have to consider the many different lanes of communication you can use.

Cutting through the traffic that consumes all these busy lanes of digital communication requires a completely different set of skills than it did 30 years ago. It requires the church to be creative in utilizing communication skills like these:

Communication in the church is no longer an administrative task. It's not confined to managing a weekly bulletin. Delivering your message effectively requires tapping into creative skills like writing, editing, video, photography, graphic design, and storytelling to creatively tell the story of what God is doing in and through your church.

Moving From One-Way to Two-Way Communication

To further complicate the communication landscape, these digital channels have a built-in expectation for the communication to be two-way, not one way. As you communicate your message across digital communication channels, you must now be prepared to receive in-bound communication from the people you're engaging with.

To not engage people as they communicate digitally with the church is today's equivalent of ignoring people as they knock on the front doors of your church.

The expectations people have for how they communicate with churches and organizations are completely different than they were 30 years ago. These changes require us to rethink and rework communication in the church so we can engage with people in person and digitally.

Physical and Digital

Don't miss this. Thirty years ago, the primary communication methods (services and print) depended on people attending church for you to be able to communicate with them. That means if someone attended your church, you effectively had one hour to communicate with and engage them.

Today, with methods such as websites, apps, social media, email, and text, you have multiple ways to communicate with and engage people during the 167 hours of the week outside of the church service.

Instead of having to wait for people to "come to you," we now have the communication tools to "go to them" and reach people digitally.

The average person who attends your church may only physically attend eight to 10 times a year. The average person your church is trying to communicate with is on social media 116 minutes a day.[3]

With the communication shifts that have happened in our culture, we have to both engage people when they attend church (physically) and as they live their lives throughout the week (digitally).

The playbook to do that is far different now than it used to be, and requires physical and digital communication to work in conjunction with each other.

So what would the path look like for someone in your community to do something as simple as Googling "God" and then actually connect with your church?

Case Study: Digital to Physical

I recently saw the impact of digital and physical engagement and how they work together when we filmed one of my all-time favorite stories at West Ridge Church.

Mike and Stephanie had been out of church for a long time. Their journey began to change one day when Stephanie, at a time of desperation, got on her computer and Googled the word "God."

Through her Google search, she stumbled upon westridge.com (our church website). Too nervous to step inside the walls of a church again, she started watching the sermons on our website—for six months. She continued checking out our church from a distance without ever stepping inside our church.

After staying connected with us online, Stephanie took the next step and visited our church in person. Once she saw how big our church was, she told her husband they could attend without being noticed.

"We're going to church next Sunday," Stephanie said.

A week later Mike and Stephanie sat in the back row through the whole service. That very Sunday, Stephanie accepted Jesus as her Savior, and everything changed.

The next Sunday, they sat closer. Then closer. Each Sunday, God was working on their hearts. From there, they took their next step into joining a small group, serving on a team, and calling our church home.

Mike and Stephanie's story didn't start at the front door of our church building. The front door for them was a website.

"Ministry is no longer just happening in four walls, it's happening at URLs." - Nona Jones, who leads Facebook's Global Faith-Based Partnerships

---

The new reality for the church is that the primary communication opportunities you have are outside the church, not inside.

Both are important and feed into each other more than ever before. The front door to your church is no longer just a physical address. The front door to your church may be your website, Facebook page, or Instagram feed.

Engaging people digitally doesn't cheapen what you're doing inside your church. It enhances it.

You've got a highway of tools God has given you to communicate the greatest message ever. How can you grab the attention of the people you're communicating with? The next section covers the new reality of attention in the church.

Discuss

- Which lanes of communication are working best for your church right now?

- Which lanes need the most work? What would need to change to be more effective?

- For people who are not attending each week physically, how are you engaging with them digitally?

- What are one to two things you can start doing now to engage people with your message during the 167 hours a week they're not in church?

3
ATTENTION

THE AVERAGE ATTENTION
SPAN OF A GOLDFISH?
9 SECONDS.

THE AVERAGE ATTENTION
SPAN OF PEOPLE IN 2018?
8 SECONDS.[4]

On April 17, 2018, at the front of a Boeing 737 plane, a casual announcement was made as passengers were preparing to fly from New York to Dallas. Just like any other day before takeoff, the flight attendant took the intercom, asked for everyone's attention, and announced the safety procedures.

A few passengers paid attention to the safety announcement. The overwhelming majority on the plane did not.

Twenty minutes into the flight, something tragic took place. A fan blade broke in one of the engines. The debris from the fan blade hit the side of the plane, shattering one of the windows, and causing absolute chaos.

The passengers were asked to do one simple thing: Put the oxygen masks on, just as they were instructed to do in the safety announcement before the plane took off.

But pictures taken during the incident revealed that most of the passengers did not put their oxygen masks on correctly. They were placing the masks over just their mouth, not their mouth and nose, as they were instructed to do.

But most of the passengers weren't listening. The announcement was spoken, but it wasn't heard.

Bobby Laurie
@BobbyLaurie

PEOPLE: Listen to your flight attendants! ALMOST EVERYONE in this photo from @SouthwestAir #SWA1380 today is wearing their mask WRONG. Put down the phone, stop with the selfies.. and LISTEN. **Cover your NOSE & MOUTH. #crewlife #psa #listen #travel #news #wn1380

2:14 PM - Apr 17, 2018

♡ 19.8K   ♡ 12.6K people are talking about this

The important safety information every person needed to know was clearly communicated in the safety announcements. Still, most people didn't get the message. Some people were distracted with a book or their phone. Others were not paying attention. Some people just tuned out the announcements because they'd heard them before.

It turns out there are a lot of things fighting for our attention. What's said isn't always heard.

Information Overload

In today's culture, there are more things fighting for our attention than ever before. Everywhere we go, we are bombarded by advertisements, messages, images, videos, and agendas that are all fighting for the valuable commodity of our sole attention.

That's an insane amount of information to process! And with each year that goes by, there's even more.

The average person you communicate with is already seeing up to 10,000 branded messages every single day.[5]

How are we responding to all the information overload we face every single day? We're fighting back. We're tuning out. Our attention span is shorter than a goldfish's, and we're only giving our attention to the messages that add value to our lives and meet a need we have.

That presents a challenge for us in the church, because everything we communicate first requires the attention of those we're communicating with. If the people you're communicating with have an average attention span of eight seconds, how intentional are you being with those first eight seconds of communication?

3 Things We Can No Longer Assume When We Communicate

1. Stop assuming you have your audience's attention. Earn it.

To earn the attention of your audience so your message is heard, focus on how you will you *capture* and *keep* their attention, instead of assuming you already have it.

Just because you said it, does not mean your audience heard it. If you're a parent, you know this to be true. I can tell my son Ethan not to hang on every table in the house like monkey bars, but a few days later when my wife called me at work saying "I'll meet you at the urgent care, Ethan pulled a table down on himself," it becomes clear to me that just because I said it, does not mean he heard it.

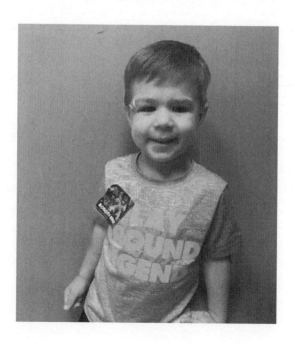

For the record, this isn't just a toddler issue. We can all be guilty of this. My wife would be the first to tell you that while I'm watching my favorite NFL football team on Sunday, the Cincinnati Bengals, she can't assume she has my attention when she tells me to take out the trash. She has to be very intentional about how she captures and keeps my attention while the game is on.

If you stop making the dangerous assumption that you already have the attention of your audience, you'll be far more intentional about how you can capture and keep their attention.

2. Stop assuming that because it's important to you, it's important to your audience. Speak first to what's important to them.

The challenge church staff and leaders deal with is the curse of knowledge. We can't help but think like insiders. We're invested in our mission and our message. As a result, the way we communicate is too often built on the assumption that since we care about our message, so will our audience.

As a response to the information overload we all face, we have developed a survival mechanism to filter the messages we receive. We filter messages through the question: "What's in it for me?" That may sound harsh and selfish, but it's the new reality for how our audience filters the more than 10,000 messages they receive each day.

My favorite author says it this way:

"Doesn't matter if you think it's important. It matters if your audience thinks it's important." -Seth Godin

Do you want to capture the attention of your audience and make those first eight seconds count? Start by speaking to the felt need your audience has, and address why it's important to them.

3. Stop adding to your message. Start simplifying.

When you're frustrated with the engagement and response your message is getting, what do you do? Most churches assume the communication issue is that the audience needs *more*. They talk longer, give more information, speak louder, make the font bigger, and add *more*.

The problem with more is the people you're communicating with are already overwhelmed by the messages and agendas they're receiving each day.

You lose attention when you continue to add more. When you add more, you're trading more work for you for more work for each person you're communicating with. Instead of adding more, do the hard work of finding the simplicity in the message you're communicating.

If you want your message to cut through the noise, you'll need to stop adding and start simplifying.

Attention can never be assumed and must always be earned.

You've got eight seconds to capture and keep someone's attention.
Stop assuming you have your audience's attention. Earn it.
Stop assuming that because it's important to you, it's important to them. Speak first to what's important to your audience.
Stop adding to your message. Start simplifying.

Your message is too important to get lost in the noise of complexity. For your message to be heard, it's going to take more intentionality than ever before to determine how you capture and keep the attention of those who you're communicating with.

Discuss

- Outside the church, how are you personally dealing with all the messages competing for your attention?

- What impact is the low attention span of your audience having in your communication as a church?

- What areas of your communication need to be simplified so you can do more with less?

THE MESSAGE AND THE MEGAPHONE

Rethinking the role of communication in the church.

What could the impact be if your message had a megaphone? A megaphone to amplify your message to reach more people in new places?

There are thousands of churches trying to get their message out there more effectively. What's holding them back?

The message is not the problem. The problem is that the message doesn't have a megaphone.

For some churches, the megaphone is broken.
For others, the megaphone doesn't exist.

Before we walk through how to communicate any message from your church, it's important to speak to the foundational ministry of communication. That's right, I said *ministry*.

Let me explain...

4

THE
MINISTRY OF
COMMUNICATION

I HAVE GIVEN ABILITY TO ALL THE SKILLED WORKERS TO MAKE EVERYTHING I HAVE COMMANDED YOU.

EXODUS 31:6

Through the last decade, I've had a chance to speak to, coach, and consult with hundreds of church leaders who are working hard to reach more people with their message.

I've met some inspiring ministry leaders serving in roles such as senior pastor, executive pastor, student pastor, children's director, and more. These ministry leaders are desperate to figure out how they can get the message of the church out to more people.

Along the way, I've also met many communication and creative leaders working in the church. These men and women are dedicating their lives to be a megaphone to the messages of their church. They may have job titles like communication director, creative director, writer, graphic designer, video director, social media manager, and many, many more. Some of these people are staff members, but many are volunteers. You won't see most of these behind-the-scenes leaders on the stage. They're using communication channels such as Facebook, Instagram, Twitter, YouTube, bulletins, websites and more. They're using their skills in writing, design, video, and photography.

As a creative arts pastor, there's a burden I carry as I look across the landscape of the church.

For far too long, too many churches have seen communication as a service department instead of a ministry.

The people with the megaphone are being boxed into the role of a service department. The role of communication is treated like a 15-minute oil change service department. "Here's my message. Here's what I want you to do with it. Here's what I want it to look like. Go promote it as quickly as you can, to as many people as you can, as cheaply as you can."

When we treat the people with the megaphone like a service department, what we're actually doing is robbing them of the ministry God has called them to. We turn creative missionaries into mindless automatons.

The message and the megaphone are meant to work in partnership together. We get glimpses of this early on in the Bible.

One of my favorite pictures of this is seeing how God used Moses and Aaron. God had a message to share through Moses. But Moses felt very inadequate to share it. Moses was confident in the message but didn't feel he had the communication skills to deliver the message. As he put it, "I am slow of speech and tongue." When Moses asked God to use someone else, God sent Moses someone else. God sent Moses a partner in his brother, Aaron.

> "What about your brother, Aaron the Levite? I know he can speak well. He is already on his way to meet you, and he will be glad to see you. You shall speak to him and put words in his mouth; I will help both of you speak and will teach you what to do. He will speak to the people for you, and it will be as if he were your mouth and as if you were God to him."
> -Exodus 4:14-16

Moses had a message.
Aaron had a megaphone.

Just like that, in the second book of the Bible, you find Aaron named the first communication director for Pastor Moses.

We get another beautiful picture of God's plan a few chapters later. God sent Moses more people to be the megaphone to the message that God gave Moses.

> "Then the Lord said to Moses, 'See, I have chosen Bezalel son of Uri, the son of Hur, of the tribe of Judah, and I have filled him with the Spirit of God, with wisdom, with understanding, with knowledge and with all kinds of skills—to make artistic designs for work in gold, silver, and bronze, to cut and set stones, to work in wood, and to engage in all kinds of crafts. Moreover, I have appointed Oholiab son of Ahisamak, of the tribe of Dan,

to help him. Also I have given ability to all the skilled workers to make everything I have commanded you.'"
-Exodus 31:1-6

God chose people like Bezalel and Oholiab and other skilled workers to be the megaphone behind the message of God. A megaphone to tell the story of what God was doing in new places and in new ways.

God is still in the business of choosing people, to fill with the Spirit of God, with wisdom, understanding, knowledge, and all kinds of skills, to put God on display.

So here we are, at a crossroads of culture, where we have countless new opportunities to put God on display with our message. Now we need the message and the megaphone to work together and amplify the message to new people in new places.

Check this out: At West Ridge Church, between July 2017 and June 2018, we had an average weekly attendance of 4,302 people. We had the opportunity to share our message in-person with 4,302 people.

Through the digital communication tools we utilize, we were able to put a megaphone on our messages and reach people who were not able to be there in-person.

My creative team used digital communication tools with a ministry mindset and saw this kind of impact:

- 84,889 visitors to our website (1,632 weekly average).
- 10 million impressions through our Facebook Page (192,307 weekly average).
- 991,700 video views on Facebook.
- 28,140 message podcasts/videos watched online (541 weekly average).
- 13,518 sermons watched online.

We have only begun to tap the surface of the potential for communicating our message across digital communication channels. In fact, each week we preach to more people on social media than our pastor does on Sunday.

These are uncharted waters for the church. Never before have we had communication tools like these to be a megaphone to our message. The message is just as important as ever. However, the megaphone that gets that message out to new places and meets people where they are, is more critical than ever before.

I don't know if you resonate more with the role of the "message" or the "megaphone." Whether you are the one driving the message or the one holding the megaphone, we all have one thing in common: We all love the church and want to see Jesus transform the lives of others just like he transformed our lives.

Communication is more than promotion.

Communication is more than an administrative task or a service department.

Communication is all about putting Jesus on display everywhere with everything you communicate.

For the church to leverage the greatest communication opportunities we've had in generations, it's going to take the message and the megaphone working together. It's going to take pastors, ministry leaders, communication leaders, and creatives partnering together by using their unique gifts to share the message of Jesus. It's going to take rethinking the role of communication in the church as a ministry, not a service department.

Discuss

- Does communication at your church look more like a service department or a ministry?

- What are some next steps you could take to rethink the role of communication in your church as a ministry?

- What would need to look different for your church to have those with the message and those with the megaphone collaborate and partner together more effectively?

COMMUNICATION PLAYBOOK

You've got a message to communicate.
What happens next?

Pop quiz.

Question #1:
What's a message your church communicated last week?
Events, programs, initiatives, or next steps?

Question #2:
What was your process for communicating that message?
Planning, strategy, timeline, language, methods of communication.

Question #3:
Was your communication effective?
Did your communication accomplish what you were hoping for?

Communication is happening every single week at your church. It's a play we run over and over again.

Attend _____.
Serve at _____.
Give to _____.
Join a _____.
Sign up for _____.

What's interesting is that the vast majority of church leaders I coach and consult are frustrated with the chaos that surrounds weekly communication.

Despite having seven days every week and 52 Sundays every year, many churches still find themselves lacking an intentional rhythm and process for how they communicate all their micro messages.

Why are so few churches intentional about a process that happens every week?

The Chaos Cycle

What's holding so many churches back from effective communication is what I call the "chaos cycle."

Here are some of the common symptoms of the chaos cycle:

- Constantly overwhelmed keeping up with tasks.
- Lack of margin for creativity.
- Reactive workflow instead of proactive planning.
- Behind schedule.
- Everything comes together at the last minute.
- No time to create systems and processes.

I'm no stranger to the chaos cycle—I've lived in it before. My first two years as a communication director of West Ridge Church were defined by this chaos cycle. On most days, I was waking up early or staying up late trying to keep my head above water, nearly drowning with all the tasks and responsibilities. Meetings consumed half my day, while the other half was spent sitting at my desk behind ever-growing piles of last-minute communication needs. It didn't take long for this chaos cycle to put me on the edge of burnout.

God still moved and incredible things still happened through our church, but I knew we were missing out on opportunities to deliver our message in new ways.

The problem we had to solve in the midst of the chaos cycle was not a message problem, but a message delivery problem. Our old way of operating and doing things no longer worked. Something needed to change.

Breaking out of the Chaos Cycle

It took too long, but I finally figured out what kept me stuck in the chaos cycle. For two weeks I conducted a personal time audit where I documented how I spent every moment of my work week. The results were startling. Everything I did and led with our communication efforts as a church was reactive, not proactive.

This became a tipping point for me to rethink everything about how we communicated as a church. What followed was a season of rethinking and refining a communication playbook that became a game changer for myself, our staff, and our church.

The Communication Playbook

In this section, I'll give you the playbook and guide you through the six plays that are essential to communicating any message in your church.

Hint: Most churches skip five of these six steps out of habit. Force yourself to go through the entire process.

Communication Playbook

1. Clarify Your Message
2. Craft Your Elevator Pitch
3. Brainstorm Creative Ideas
4. Develop Your Communication Plan
5. Execute Your Plan
6. Evaluate Your Results

As you walk through each play, try applying this playbook with a message you need to communicate in your church. Filter your message through this playbook and see what you may need to *start* doing, *stop* doing, and *continue* doing.

You have a message to communicate. What happens next?

Let's dive in and rethink how you can communicate your message.

5

CLARIFY YOUR MESSAGE

HOW TO CLARIFY YOUR MESSAGE WITH THREE QUESTIONS.

What is the first thing most churches do when they have a message to communicate?

- ✓ Announce it from the stage.
- ✓ Print it in the bulletin.
- ✓ Put up signs.
- ✓ Email the church.
- ✓ Add it to the website.
- ✓ Share it on social media.

Most churches jump straight to the promotion phase when they have a message to communicate. When we jump straight to promoting our message, we make the mistake of assuming the message we're communicating is as clear to our audience as it is to us.

Through this first step in the communication playbook, I want to challenge you to rethink what you do first when you have a message to communicate. I want to challenge you to clarify your message before you start promoting it.

Clarifying your message starts by asking the right questions instead of assuming you already have the right answers.

I'll show you how you can clarify your message with three clarifying questions.

Three Clarifying Questions

"Give me six hours to cut down a tree and I'll spend the first four sharpening my axe."
-Abraham Lincoln

The first thing you should do before communicating your message externally is sharpen your message internally. Your message needs to be crystal clear before you begin communicating it.

The first step of the communication playbook is to clarify your message by filtering it through these three questions:

1. Who is your target audience?
2. What's the win for your message?
3. What are the barriers to your message?

There's nothing super unique about these questions. You've likely heard them (or something similar) before. While these questions are simple, they are extremely powerful because they force you to abandon any assumptions you may be making about your message.

I'm not exaggerating when I tell you I use these questions every day in my role as a creative arts pastor. These questions have become a filter for how I think and approach anything we do as a church.

The clarity you get from each of these questions will be essential to every other step along the way in the communication playbook.

Next, I'll dive into each of these powerful questions and show you a triangle visual I use every week in my work with the church.

Clarifying Question #1:
Who Is Your Target Audience?

You   Target Audience

With this question you want to identify:

• What are you noticing about the attendance patterns in your congregation?

Who Is Your Target Audience?

The very first thing you should clarify for your message is to define who your message is for. Is your message for adults? Married couples? Men? Women? Parents? Students? Kids? A particular neighborhood?

Everything you do from this point forward hinges on reaching your target audience with your message. Get specific about your target audience. The more niche the audience, the more targeted and strategic your communication can be to reach them. The broader your audience, the harder it is for your message to be relevant enough to capture their attention.

There's no magic strategy that universally works to reach every audience. The tactics will need to change based on the target audience. We know that we would communicate differently to a middle school student than an older adult. Every target audience is unique, and deserves to be treated as such. We all know this intuitively, but we don't always apply it with our communication strategy in the church.

As you clarify the target audience for your message, it will help you identify two things:

❑ Identify a target persona.

There are times when your message legitimately is for "everyone." When that happens, you need a target persona to help guide your decisions for how to communicate your message.

A target persona is a specific type of person or demographic that best represents the target audience for your message. When you hit the specific target persona, you're more likely to reach the broader audience you're trying to reach.

For example, at West Ridge Church, when we have a message we're trying to communicate with adults, we pick a target persona of a 34-year-old mechanic. For kids' ministry communication, we have a target persona of a fifth grade boy. That target persona becomes a filter for how we approach the various messages we communicate as a church.

We've found that if we build our communication strategy around reaching that target persona, we have a good chance of reaching the rest of our audience. When we communicate with adults, if we reach the 34-year-old mechanic, we're likely to reach the broader audience that makes up our church and community. For kids, if we reach the fifth grade boy, we're more likely to reach the entire span of elementary aged kids, as opposed to if we used a second grade boy as our target persona.

❏ **Identify the best communication channels for engaging your target audience with your message.**
Thirty years ago, you could reach the vast majority of your audience by using in-person communication channels like print and stage announcements.

It's not so simple anymore.

The communication channels you use to deliver your message should be based around the communication channels your target audience is actively engaging.

Let's say the target audience for your message is high school students. If that's the case, you'll want to identify the communication channels high school students are already using and reach them there. As you research, you may find that email and print may not be effective for reaching high school students, but social media and texting could be your go-to methods.

As you research the best communication channels for your target audience, be sure to identify both digital and physical channels.

One Last Tip for Understanding Your Target Audience

Want to do something that will be a game changer for understanding your target audience? Find and speak with individuals who are in your target audience. Spend some time with them. Ask them questions so you can better understand who they are, what they need, and how to reach them. Spending time with people from your target audience, especially if you don't personally fit in this audience, will help you build a more objective perspective on the people you're trying to reach and build empathy for where they're coming from.

Action Step: Who's Your Target Audience?

- Identify who the target audience is for your message.
- Identify which communication channels are best for engaging that target audience.

Clarifying Question #2: What's the Win?

Win

You

Target Audience

With this question you want to identify:

- What are you noticing about the attendance patterns in your congregation?

What's the Win?

Back in 2016 during the Rio Olympics, I watched the sport of archery for the first time. Each athlete went through an intentional process as they took up their bow and arrows and prepared to shoot. They would lock their eyes on the target, aim, and shoot. After each shot, they'd take a closer look to see if they hit their target and make any necessary adjustments for the next shot. The process was clear from beginning to end. Every action focused on one thing—hitting the bullseye.

What if your communication strategy looked more like the archer's process?

The entire communication process, from beginning to end, should be about accomplishing the win of your message.

With the chaos cycle of all the things to communicate in the church, it can be all too easy to communicate a message without knowing what you're actually trying to accomplish.

You need to aim at a target.

Before you start shooting arrows, you must first lock your eyes on the target by clarifying what the win is for your message so you can focus

85

everything you do on hitting your target.

To clarify the win, you can't just think of this from the perspective of you as the church. You have to wear the hat of your audience as well. We'll clarify the win by asking clarifying questions through three perspectives:

- What's the win for you as a church?
- What's the win for your target audience?
- Is this a shared win for you and your audience?

What's the Win for You as a Church?

What are you trying to accomplish through communicating your message? The answer to that question is your win.

When you identify the win for your message as a church, you can aim your whole communication strategy at hitting your target and accomplishing that win. But if you don't know the target before you start delivering your message, you're just shooting blind. You'll waste lots of arrows on the off chance that one of them finds the target.

Your church's win may look something like filling in the blanks for these statements:

- ❏ We want to accomplish _____.
- ❏ The problem we're trying to solve is _____.
- ❏ The ministry purpose and objective is _____?
- ❏ The next step we want our audience to take is _____.

Some of the biggest misses I've experienced through the years in creative ministry have been at the cost of not having clarity over what I was trying to accomplish before I started communicating a message. This happens most often when there's a last-minute "urgent" message and no time to clarify it. I've found that when our message win is unclear, our communication is information rich and inspiration poor.

After you clarify the win for your church, you have to take off your hat as a church leader and filter your message through the perspective of your target audience.

What's the Win for Your Target Audience?

Many churches fall into a trap when they communicate. It's an easy trap to fall into. The trap is that they're only thinking about their message from the perspective of a staff member or insider, instead of the perspective of the target audience for the message.

Think about the advertisements and commercials that grab your attention and resonate with you. Are they the ones that focus on themselves? Or are they the ones that speak to a problem you need to solve and call you to action?

Don't fall for the trap of making your message all about you as the church. Clarify what the win is for your target audience, and focus the delivery of your message around helping them accomplish that win.

To inspire action, your communication strategy has to focus on how your message will help your target audience accomplish their win.

Take a moment to think about your message from the perspective of your target audience:

- Why should they care about your message?
- What felt need will your message resolve?
- What's in it for them?
- What would be different if they responded to your message?

Before you go any further, there's one more question to ask.

Is This a Shared Win for the Church and Target Audience?

Take a close look at the win for you as a church and the win for your target audience.

Does your message help the church and the target audience accomplish their win?

The needs of your church and your target audience must converge.

When that happens, everybody wins.

91

When that doesn't happen, your message won't connect.

If you're too focused on accomplishing your own win, but don't resolve a personal felt need or conflict for your target audience, you're going to miss. That disconnect means you can't reach your audience. You could have the biggest budget or the most brilliant idea, but you'll still miss if you don't get that shared win.

Now you could take a page out of the typical political playbook and spin your message as something that will help your target audience experience their win.

But that's no good. You need an authentic win.

Trying to spin a message into a win will do more harm than good. It will break down trust between your church and the people you're trying to reach.

Case Study: Small Groups

Let's take a look at how this could be applied through communicating a message about small groups.

Message: Sign up to join a small group.
Target Audience: Adults in the church.
Church Win: 50 new people join small groups to make more disciples in our church.
Target Audience Win: Community and friendships with others.

Which of these two options would be more effective in challenging adults in the church to get connected in a small group?

> Option 1: "Church, we have a goal of getting 50 new people involved in small groups in our church. Sign up today to get started in a small group and grow as a disciple."

> Option 2: "You weren't meant to do life on your own. Life is better together. There's a place for you in a small group, where you can experience community and build friendships as you grow to become a more fully devoted follower of Jesus."

Adults would be less likely to respond to communication built around the church meeting an internal goal (engaging 50 new people in small groups). However, they would give their attention and respond to a message that speaks to the need they have of community and friendship within the church.

The message and ministry of small groups can be a solution to both the church and the target audience. What I've often found is that the messages we communicate in the church often bridge the gap between an emotional felt need of our target audience and their true spiritual need. Meeting the felt need for adults of community and friendship is a bridge to the church's win of making more disciples. It's a shared win.

———

The words you use must speak to the needs of your target audience and point them to your message. The next section will cover overcoming barriers to that message.

Action Step: What's the Win?

- Define the win for the church.

- Define the win for the target audience.

- Identify if your message is a shared win for the church and target audience.

Clarifying Question #3:
What Are the Barriers?

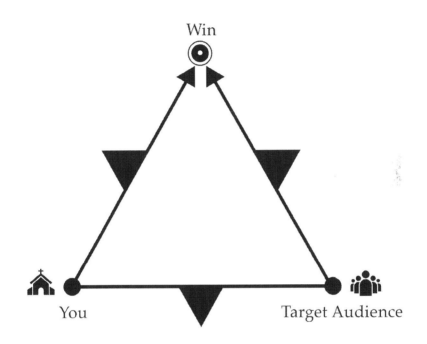

With this question you want to identify:

- Barriers between you and your audience.

- Barriers between you and the win.

- Barriers between your audience and the win.

Every message you communicate will need to overcome barriers. If you want people to sign up, show up, share, give, or take any type of next step, you'll need to remove barriers that keep people from taking a next step to respond to your message.

Most churches don't identify barriers that get in the way until after they've communicated their message. That's way too late.

When you identify the barriers before you start communicating your message, you can be proactive about addressing those barriers with your strategy so they don't keep you from accomplishing your win.

There are three distinct barriers that need to be clarified for your message:

- Barriers between you and your audience.
- Barriers between you and the win.
- Barriers between your audience and the win.

What Are the Barriers Between You and Your Audience?

□ **Identify how your audience perceives the church.**

What's your perception of a car salesperson? Based on past experience and common perception, you're likely to walk into any car dealer assuming the salesperson is thinking about their win, not yours. You would assume you can't always trust what they have to say. Like it or not, that's the brand of the car salesperson. The best car salesperson recognizes those barriers and works hard to remove them.

Now how about the cultural perceptions of the church? If you're trying to reach young adults who are not engaged with the church, you must understand some of the barriers you'll need to overcome to reach them. According to Barna[6]:

> "More than one-third say their negative perceptions are a result of moral failures in church leadership (35%). And substantial majorities of millennials who don't go to church say they see Christians as judgmental (87%), hypocritical (85%), anti-homosexual (91%), and insensitive to others (70%)."

Based on the target audience of your message, are there any barriers you'll encounter because of their perception of the church (or your church specifically)?

The two most common barriers I see between a church and their audience can be summed up in two words: trust and authenticity.

❑ **Identify any trust issues your audience has with the church.**
Most people assume anyone communicating a message has an agenda. Since this is the default position of so many people we communicate with, it's critical we communicate our message with authenticity. Your audience needs to know why you care about your message, and they need to trust that you have their best interest in mind.

Does your target audience trust what you have to say? Will they suspect you have an agenda?

❑ **Identify where your church needs to build trust with your audience.**
Many of the communication barriers churches face are universal. But there are likely some barriers unique to your situation. Maybe you're a contemporary church in a traditional community. Maybe your church has a history in the community—either good or bad—that colors how your community sees (or doesn't see) you.

For your church, what barriers exist between you and your audience? Identify those barriers. Then get strategic in breaking them down as you communicate your message.

What Are the Barriers Between You and Your Win?

❑ **Identify barriers that hold you back from accomplishing the win.**
Is there a clear problem or pain point you're trying to fix through the message you're communicating? If so, identify the barriers keeping you from solving that problem.

❑ **Identify barriers you have in clarifying and simplifying your message.**
You may have only eight seconds to grab the attention of your audience. To do that, you have to overcome the barrier of complexity. If your

message doesn't feel clear and simple to you, chances are it won't feel clear and simple to your audience.

A visitor card is a good example of something that needs to be stupid simple. And you might have a hard time seeing potential complications because you're in the know. It's key to get outside of your own perspective and see things the way your target audience sees them.

❏ **Identify barriers you've encountered in the past when communicating your message.**
Think back to the last time you communicated this message or similar messages. The best lessons from the future can often come from lessons learned in the past. Most churches work on a cyclical calendar and at the very least Christmas and Easter come every year, so look at previous years to see what worked and what didn't. Make note of those barriers you've experienced in the past so you can solve them in the future.

❏ **Identify tasks or milestones that must happen for you to accomplish your win.**
What steps or tasks are mission critical to communicate your message effectively? For your message to connect, it may be dependent on a certain communication deliverable, like a video, stage announcement, or social media campaign.

If you can't accomplish your win without a specific task or by hitting a certain milestone, be sure to identify that in the early stages so it doesn't become a barrier.

What Are the Barriers Between Your Target Audience and Their Win?

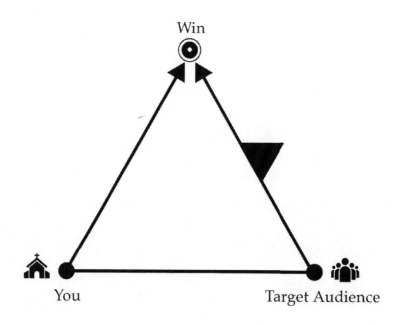

❏ **Identify barriers that keep your audience from responding to your message.**

With every program, event, or new initiative, there are barriers that need to be overcome. There are barriers such as the high cost of registration, the need to take time off from work, childcare, complex instructions, and information overload.

Many times, you can remove those barriers before you ever communicate your message. If you can't, it's vital to identify and speak to those barriers so your audience knows how to overcome them.

For example, if you're asking people to sign up for a missions trip, the biggest barrier your audience experiences is likely raising support. If that's the case, speak to that specific barrier as you communicate your message. Help people overcome that barrier by giving them ideas, tools, and resources for raising support.

No matter what your job title is, you have a role to play in identifying and removing barriers that keep people from taking their next step.

❏ **Identify barriers you encountered in the past when you communicated this message.**
How did people respond the last time you communicated this message? What didn't work? What was missing? What was confusing?

A few years back at West Ridge Church we wanted everyone to fill out a small survey during the service. We had done this same survey the year before, and a simple barrier kept our audience from responding: They needed pens.

Most people don't bring a pen to church. By identifying this from the past, we were able to proactively fix it. We handed out pens as people came into the service as well as provided a digital version of the survey they could fill out with their phones. By adding pens and a digital version of the survey, we saw exponentially more people respond. All it took was removing a simple barrier.

❑ **Identify barriers your target audience may experience in the timing of your message.**

One of the challenges we addressed earlier in the book is that people are attending and engaging very differently than they did 30 years ago. If you want your message to be heard and responded to, then it may require more time to communicate that message than it did in the past.

If you're communicating a missions trip to another country that requires raising support, you need months of lead time before that missions trip ever takes place.

Think through how much time your audience needs to be able to hear and respond to your message.

———

Case Study: Small Groups

At West Ridge Church, this question of "what are the barriers" has been a game changer for building creative strategies to communicate our message.

Before we communicated the message of getting connected in a small group to the adults in our church, one of the members of our Connections Team staff, Rodney Hunt, went to Facebook to ask a question:

> "If you have been asked to join a small group at your church and weren't able to do so, what were the reasons? What are the barriers that keep you from joining a small group?"

This simple Facebook post received 116 comments and gave us some very insightful feedback. Through the feedback from that post and from other conversations we've had with people in our church, we found that the top two barriers keeping people from getting connected to a group were convenience/busyness and childcare.

By clarifying our audience, the win, and the barriers for the message of getting connected in a small group, we quickly had the foundation of what it would take for our message to connect with our audience.

We shared stories of people who thought they were too busy but found that getting into a small group was worth their time. We communicated that many of our small groups meet at the church where we're able to offer childcare. We communicated these stories through video, pre-service slides, social media posts, and emails.

By simply asking what barriers our target audience faced, we were able to speak to how it was worth their time and provide options for the issue of childcare.

Action Step: What Are the Barriers?

- Identify barriers between you and your target audience.

- Identify barriers between you and the win.

- Identify barriers between your audience and the win.

6

CRAFT YOUR ELEVATOR PITCH

HOW TO COMMUNICATE YOUR MESSAGE WITH A CLEAR, CONCISE, AND COMPELLING ELEVATOR PITCH.

It's the classic elevator pitch: You've got 30 seconds to share your message with a captive audience. Ready? Go!

This exercise is a standard in the business world for a reason. It forces you to cull your message to the very essence, strip away the fluff and bravado, and share the most important details that will connect with your audience.

You need to develop an elevator pitch for every message your church communicates. It will help sharpen your message, hone in on your audience, and be more effective.

"The purpose of an elevator pitch is to describe a situation or solution so compelling that the person you're with wants to hear more even after the elevator ride is over." -Seth Godin

---

Tip: Let's Be Honest
Language like "You don't want to miss this," "Join us," and "An event you'll never forget," should not be confused with an elevator pitch. Those are throwaway phrases we get stuck using when we haven't taken the time to do the hard work of crafting language that compels people to respond.

Same with exclamation marks. They often slip into our copy to compensate for a lack of clarity and compelling vision.

It's More Than a Pitch

When you communicate your message through a stage announcement, social media post, bulletin blurb, or email, you only have a brief moment to capture the attention of your audience and move them to action (eight-second attention span, remember?). Every single word you use matters.

The stakes are too high and your message is too important for you not to be intentional with the brief moments you have to deliver your message.

I've found that the time you invest in crafting your elevator pitch can have the biggest return of anything you do in the communication process. This exercise helps you develop the message strategy you can use throughout all of your communication channels.

For example, the elevator pitch you craft could impact:

- How you talk about your message at a worship service with a stage announcement.
- Ways you grab someone's attention on a social media post.
- Words you use to communicate your message on your website or in a bulletin announcement.

Here's the good news. If you've filtered your message through the three clarifying questions in the last section, you've already done the hardest part of crafting your elevator pitch.

So what are the elements of a great elevator pitch?

A Great Elevator Pitch Consists of Four Things:

1. Target Audience
A clear and specific group of people you are communicating with.

2. Problem to Solve
A felt need or barrier that connects with your target audience.

3. Solution
Your message and how that will add value to your target audience.

4. Next Step
A clear call to action for what to do next.

Elevator Pitch Examples

Want to see what an elevator pitch could look like? Here are a few we recently developed at West Ridge Church.

Elevator pitch for an event called Marriage Connect:

> *"Marriage is tough. But it's worth it. If you are married or preparing to be, take two hours to invest in your relationship and attend Marriage Connect. There's no cost, and childcare is available. Sign up now at _____."*

Let's deconstruct this message so you can see how this developed:

- Target audience = People who are married or preparing to be.
- Problem to solve = Marriage is tough and worth investing in.
- Solution = Attend our event called Marriage Connect.
- Next step = Sign up online for free.

As we put this together, it was important for us to identify and remove three of the biggest barriers to people taking their next step: time, cost, and childcare.

Here's another example for a discipleship environment we have in our church called Next Steps.

Elevator pitch for Next Steps:

"Whether you've been a Christian for five days or five decades, everyone has a next step they can take to grow in their faith. Find your next step with your faith and your church in our four week environment called Next Steps. Visit westridge.com/nextsteps to sign up."

Here's a breakdown of this elevator pitch:

- Target audience = Anyone who is following Jesus and wants to grow in their faith.
- Problem to solve = Discover what their next step is for growing in their faith.
- Solution = Attend Next Steps.
- Next Step = Sign up online for free.

The playbook for crafting your elevator pitch is simpler than it might seem at first. I've found that once you clarify your message, you have all the tools you need to develop a compelling elevator pitch that will grab the attention of your target audience.

Two Things You Should Do When Developing Your Elevator Pitch

As you craft your message elevator pitch, I'd encourage you to do two things:

1. Try Multiple Drafts

It's extremely rare for your first draft to be your best draft. I can't think of one time when we landed on our best elevator pitch on the first try. It may take a few drafts to find something that sticks, so don't be afraid to try a few different directions.

2. Test Your Pitch on Someone

The best way to see how effective your pitch is, is to pitch it to someone! Nothing tests how effective your elevator pitch is like having to communicate it to someone in your target audience. Try the elevator pitch on a few people who will give you honest feedback, and make adjustments until you land on something that is effective. As you try your pitch on someone, pay close attention to the words and phrases that grab their attention. Trust me, it's much better to hear from a friend or trusted coworker that your elevator pitch is awful—as opposed to hearing it from your entire congregation when it's far too late to do anything about it.

The time and energy you put into crafting your elevator pitch is worth it. Remember, you've only got a brief moment to capture and keep the attention of your audience. Make it count.

Action Step: Craft Your Elevator Pitch

- Take a message you need to communicate right now and try developing an elevator pitch.

- Test your elevator pitch on someone who fits the target audience for your message.

- After you give the pitch, give them permission to share their honest feedback. Ask them things like:

  - Did this grab your attention?

  - How did this make you feel?

  - What questions would you have after hearing that?

7

BRAINSTORM CREATIVE IDEAS

HOW TO COLLABORATE ON IDEAS THAT CREATIVELY COMMUNICATE YOUR MESSAGE.

Once you've clarified your message and crafted your elevator pitch, it's time to brainstorm how you can creatively communicate your message.

In the digital age, you can't assume you already have the attention of your audience. The best way to earn attention in today's culture is through creativity.

Creativity, and especially the creative process, can be overwhelming and mystical to a lot of people. If that's you, let me take a moment to demystify what creativity truly is.

Creativity = problem solving. It's that simple.

Creativity isn't mystical—it's practical. But it does require practice.

Stephen Brewster, one of the most creative people I know, says "Creativity is more muscle than magic." Creativity is a muscle you have to exercise. The more you use it, the stronger it becomes.

The goal of a creative brainstorm is to collaborate on ideas that help you do three things:

1. Engage your target audience.

2. Overcome barriers.

3. Accomplish the win of your message.

You've already done the hard work of clarifying the target audience, barriers, and win of your message. Now it's time to get creative.

The Three Phases of a Creative Brainstorm

Creativity can happen in isolation, but it's far more powerful in collaboration.

I've learned a lot of lessons through running literally hundreds of creative brainstorm meetings. Let me tell you, creative brainstorm meetings can be messy. But they're worth it.

Here's my playbook for a creative brainstorm, including what to do before, during, and after each session.

1. Before the Brainstorm

❑ **Invite participants.**
Decide who needs to be at the brainstorm. This could include the key message stakeholders, leaders, people who are helping execute the creative ideas, or people who think creatively and would add value to the conversation.

As you consider who to invite, I'd encourage you to get a room full of dreamers. Creative brainstorms are most effective when you have a room full of people focused on dreaming new ideas. The "dreamers" and the "doers" are both critical for the communication process. However,

I've learned that in the early stages of the brainstorming process, you need people who are saying "what if we did _____" instead of "how will we do ____?"

Send out a calendar invite, giving all participants a clear time and place. If you can, find a fun, bright, creative place to do your brainstorm. Get out of the office if you can. It's hard to get creative when you're surrounded by cubicles.

Don't forget to plan for what I consider the only non-negotiable for any creative meeting: coffee.

❑ **Send out a message brief, detailing what you're communicating.** In the days, or preferably weeks, leading up to your brainstorm, send the participants a brief of what you're trying to accomplish with this meeting.

Outline what you know about your message:

- What's your message?
- Who's the target audience?
- What's the win? What are you trying to accomplish?
- What are the barriers you need to address?

Then invite them to come prepared with ideas and inspiration that would help you connect with your target audience, remove barriers, and accomplish the win for your message.

Want to know how to make your meeting more creative and productive? Give participants clarity of your message and time to generate ideas before they arrive at the meeting. The best creative ideas are rarely spontaneous and usually become refined and processed over time. Give your participants the clarity and time they need to brainstorm creative ideas.

2. During the Brainstorm

❑ **Establish the rules.**

Your participants are probably wondering questions like: When will the meeting end? Are we taking a break? Can I step out, stand up, or walk around if that helps me brainstorm? Are we just brainstorming ideas, or will we talk about what we will execute in this meeting?

Set the tone for what participants can expect by establishing the rules for the meeting.

❑ **Talk through the message brief and elevator pitch.**

Before you start brainstorming ideas, make sure everyone is on the same page and has a clear understanding of the message, the audience, the barriers, and the win.

Have the message brief and elevator pitch printed out or in plain sight on a whiteboard or TV for everyone to see. Quickly go over the message and invite people to ask any questions they may have.

As you cover the message brief and elevator pitch, invite participants to put on the hat of the target audience. Put a name or face behind the person or type of people you're trying to reach.

If your message has a target audience of unchurched adults in your community, invite every person to take a moment to write down a name of someone they know personally who fits that audience. You've now given everyone a person they can be thinking about as they brainstorm ideas to reach that person.

❑ **Brainstorm creative ideas.**
Remember, creativity is just problem solving. During the brainstorm phase, collaborate on ideas that would solve these problems.

Look for ideas that would help you:

- Connect and engage with your target audience.
- Overcome barriers between you, your audience, and your win.
- Accomplish the win for you and your target audience.

The clarity you have around your message can filter the creative ideas generated. The participants can now focus their best ideas on solving those problems.

How you capture the creative ideas that come up in the conversation is completely up to you. My preferred method is to use a white board to map the ideas that come up during the conversation.

Another great way to get ideas flowing is a creative show and tell. Invite your participants to share creative ideas that have inspired them. The purpose is not to copy those ideas. The purpose is to borrow elements of those ideas that you can contextualize for your own needs to engage your target audience, overcome barriers, and accomplish the win of your message.

3. After the Brainstorm

❑ **Send a thank you note to the team.**
Following the meeting, take a moment to send a thank you email or handwritten note to everyone who participated in the meeting. This will help you build a culture that honors people's time and appreciates the creative ideas and input of each person.

In your encouragement, be specific and point out any ideas or contributions you appreciated. Whatever you praise and celebrate are the things that will be repeated the next time.

———

Following the creative brainstorm process, you'll need to move from the idea phase into the execution phase. That's what we'll cover next as we create a communication plan. But first, let's see how a brainstorm helped overcome a barrier and score a big win.

Case Study: Brainstorming Lights at West Ridge

In 2015, our leadership team recognized a problem we needed to solve. There were 357,000 people in a 10-mile radius of our church, and more than 88% of those people didn't have a church home and likely didn't have a relationship with Jesus.

The unique problem we were trying to solve was that despite those 357,000 people being so close to our church, they likely had no clue where we were located or who we were as a church. More importantly, many of those 357,000 people didn't know there was a church that cares for them and a God who loves them.

We knew we had a giant barrier to overcome if we were ever going to make a dent in reaching those 357,000 people.

So that led us to a creative brainstorm.

Our target audience? The 357,000 people within 10 miles of our church who didn't have a church home.

The key barriers for our target audience? They didn't know where we were located and didn't have a compelling reason to find us.

The win for our message? Any ideas that would overcome the barrier for our target audience.

We talked. We brainstormed. Most importantly, we prayed that instead of a couple good ideas we could have one big God idea. That's where Lights at West Ridge got its start.

We asked the question, "What do families in our community seek out and drive to?" The most frequent answer to that question? Christmas lights. Families love driving around during the Christmas season to check out great Christmas lights. And that's where we had an opportunity: There were very few chances locally for people to experience good Christmas lights—especially for free!

Long story short, we moved forward with creating a free Christmas lights experience called "Lights at West Ridge" during the month of December. We went all out decorating the front of our building with tens of thousands of Christmas lights, created a 15-minute light show synced with music, and developed a plan to connect with each person who drove on our campus.

This was risky. We had never done anything like this before. But for the 357,000 people at stake, it was worth it.

Through our first year of doing Lights at West Ridge, over 12,000 people from the community visited our campus. The best part about it? The vast majority said it was their first time at West Ridge.

The win wasn't people seeing Christmas lights. The win was thousands of people finding and engaging with our church for the very first time. We saw a 149% increase in first-time guests compared to the previous year. We saw countless people visit our church on a Sunday for the first time and mention that they found us after checking out Lights at West Ridge.

The creative idea didn't start with doing a Christmas light show. The creative idea started with trying to solve a compelling problem.

You never know what God can do through a creative idea.

Action Step: Brainstorm Creative Ideas

- Use this brainstorm playbook the next time you need to collaborate on creative ideas.

8

DEVELOP YOUR COMMUNICATION PLAN

HOW TO CREATE A PROACTIVE COMMUNICATION PLAN TO DELIVER YOUR MESSAGE.

"If you fail to plan, you are planning to fail." -Benjamin Franklin

By far, the most common frustrations I hear from pastors, ministry leaders, and communication leaders all point to one thing: planning ahead.

Not only is it causing frustration with everyone involved in the process, it's also the main culprit of ineffective communication.

Planning ahead isn't just helpful. It's essential. It has the potential to make or break your ability to communicate your message and engage your audience.

The time you invest in planning ahead will give you an exponential return.

Planning ahead:

- Provides time for greater creativity.
- Saves money.
- Creates margin to use digital and physical communication channels to deliver your message.
- Fosters staff health for your team and volunteers by setting them up for success and valuing their time.

Pick Two

For every message you communicate and the things you create, you can pick two of these three things:

Great	Fast	Cheap

Fast + Cheap = Not great
Great + Fast = Not cheap
Great + Cheap = Not fast

Your message is too important to have to settle for fast and cheap. Great and cheap has a price, and that cost is planning ahead.

Developing Your Communication Plan

Through clarifying your message and crafting your elevator pitch, you've established the why behind your message. That why is the foundation on which you build the rest of your strategy.

With the why in mind, you brainstormed creative ideas to capture the attention of your audience and engage them with your message.

Now it's time to develop your communication plan. You'll do that by creating a message communication plan that looks like this:

EASTER - COMMUNICATION PLAN

	In-Service	Web & Social Media	Printing & Signage	Notes
FEB 17				• Series art completed
FEB 24 SOFT LAUNCH	• Begin feature on announcement loop	• WestRidge.com/Easter published • Service times posted on social media	• Signage and invite cards sent to printer	
MAR 3	• Stage announcement	• 1-2 Social media posts		• Video promo completed and uploaded to Vimeo/ Dropbox
MAR 10 MARKETING BLITZ	• Video Promo • Interview with vision for Easter with Senior Pastor	• 3 Social media posts • Share video of Interview with Senior Pastor • Promo Video • Service Times Graphic	• Road banners at entrance • Indoor signs in atrium • Invite cards available at Help Center & Cafe • Begin feature on back of worship guide	
MAR 17	• Video Promo • Stage Announcement	• 3 Social media posts	• Invite cards passed out • Kids ministry passes out 3D Easter cards to kids	
MAR 24	• Video Promo • Pre-Service: Kids 3D Easter Promo Video • Stage Announcement	• 4-5 Social media posts	• Invite cards passed out • Kids ministry passes out 3D Easter cards to kids	• Send Easter email
MAR 29-31 EASTER SERVICES	• Announcement Video: Church app and preview of next week	• Home page focus on Easter and first-time guests • Share photos of worship experience on social media	• Easter Worship Guide: Back focused on connecting first time guests	• Photographers/ videographers capture services

Your communication plan will clarify how you'll deliver your message, from the beginning to the end. This includes:

- What you're doing to communicate your message.
- Where you deliver your message.
- When you deliver your message.
- How you execute each deliverable for your plan.

To download the free message communication plan template, visit RethinkCommunicationBook.com/resources

WHAT

What you're doing to communicate your message.

———

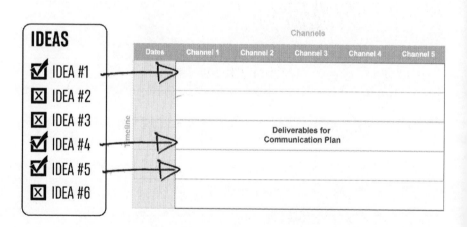

Through many years of leading creative teams, there's one statement I come back to again and again:

You can do anything. But you can't do everything.

Through the creative brainstorm process, there were probably lots of good "what if we did _____" ideas that may have been built around a video, print piece, social media, email, or any other type of communication deliverable.

Now you need to filter through the brainstorm ideas and decide what you're going to do to communicate your message. The ideas selected will become the core deliverables used to share your message and execute your communication plan.

Lots of factors go into deciding what you should do to communicate your message. Follow these two steps to filter your ideas as you develop your communication plan.

Step 1: Choose the Best Ideas for Communicating Your Message

Here are a few things you should consider as you decide what you're doing to communicate your message:

1. Choose ideas that help solve a problem.
Creativity is problem solving. It doesn't matter how simple or intricate

the idea is. What matters is if your idea will help you solve a problem.

Choose ideas that would be most effective in engaging your target audience, overcoming barriers, and accomplishing the win of your message.

There may have been some great ideas that came up in the creative brainstorm, but they don't directly help you accomplish your win. Save those ideas for another project.

2. Choose ideas that generate the most energy and excitement.
In the creative brainstorm, there are often ideas that people keep going back to. Make note of the ideas that generate the most energy, passion, and excitement. If an idea is energizing you, it's got a better chance of engaging your target audience.

3. Choose ideas that you have margin and bandwidth to execute.
Don't say yes to an idea until you know you've got the tools and resources to execute the idea. If you're not sure what it will take to execute an idea, make sure you talk to the person or people who would make this idea happen.

Sometimes an idea isn't worth the cost of the bandwidth it would require for the people making the idea happen. For everything you say yes to, you're effectively saying no to another thing the team could (or should) be doing.

Step 2: Create a List of Deliverables

After deciding the big ideas to move forward with, create a list of specific deliverables you'll need to produce.

Your list may be built around your own creative ideas for executing things like:

- In-service moments
- Videos
- Social media campaigns
- Print handouts
- Local ads

The list will drive how you plan where, when, and how you communicate your message. That's what we'll cover next.

Action Step: What You're Doing to Communicate Your Message

- From the idea list you made during the creative brainstorm, decide specifically what you are doing to communicate your message.

- Based on the ideas you're moving forward with, make a list of the specific deliverables that will need to be produced.

WHERE

Where you will communicate your message.

___

Channels				
Channel 1	Channel 2	Channel 3	Channel 4	Channel 5

After deciding what you'll do to communicate your message, the next step is to plan which communication channels you will use to deliver your message.

A communication channel is a specific place where you can deliver your message.

Here's an example of what some common communication channels look like for many churches:

Worship Services	Stage Announcement
	Pre/Post Service Slides
	Video Content
Print	Bulletin
	Invite Cards
	Signage + Outdoor Banners
	Mailers
Digital	Website
	Church App
	Email
Social Media	Facebook
	Twitter
	Instagram

The channels you use will have the biggest impact on how your message is shaped and received by your target audience. These channels can play a part in breaking down (or sometimes adding to) barriers that keep you or your audience from accomplishing their win.

What channels will help you accomplish your win and overcome the barriers in communicating your message? Would your message be best communicated through written words? Pictures? Stories? Vision from your pastor?

Based on your creative ideas and deliverables, here's how you can decide where to deliver your message:

Tips for Choosing Your Communication Channels

1. Use channels that bring your elevator pitch to life.

Your elevator pitch can help guide how your message would translate through each of the available channels in your church.

You don't have to use every channel for every message. That's a fast-track to overwhelming yourself and your audience.

By the way, I'll cover the importance of creating communication standards to filter how you use your communication channels in the last section of the book.

Case Study: What If Experiment

Recently, our team at West Ridge Church needed to communicate a generosity campaign to our church called the "What If Experiment." As we clarified our message and developed our elevator pitch, we were able to narrow in on our win. We wanted the adults of our church to hear a compelling vision around generosity, and we wanted each person in our church to take their own next step in generosity.

Following the creative brainstorm, we executed a big idea built around a creative approach to a vision video from our senior pastor. Through his communication, we wanted our church to see the impact of their giving, hear vision for being known as a generous church, and respond by making a giving commitment.

Since it was critical for this message to be communicated from our senior pastor, we built our communication strategy around the channels where we could use a vision video from our pastor. We focused the majority of our creative efforts around that one video, and shared that video in services, email, social media, and online.

The earlier stages of the communication playbook gave us clarity and helped us narrow our focus to building around that video.

Every message is unique and deserves to be treated as such. If a communication channel isn't a good fit to bring your elevator pitch to life, then don't use it and focus your energies where they will make a bigger impact.

————

2. Use channels your target audience actively engages with.
Each target audience may utilize your communication channels in different ways. That means you may need to use different channels to reach different types of audiences. Identify the channels your audience uses most frequently and engage them there.

3. Think physical and digital channels.
The new reality for many churches is that people are attending less frequently (as we covered in the *Attendance* section earlier). That means you have to be more intentional with communicating your message through digital communication. You can no longer assume that sharing your message from stage during a worship service will reach the majority of your audience.

That doesn't make your in-person communication less important. It just makes your digital communication equally as important.

Where is your target audience already engaging? Engage them with your message there.

Exercise: What Communication Channels Does Your Church Have?

Make a list of the different channels you have available at your church. This is a great exercise for you and your team to process through together.

There are benefits to writing out all of your church's communication channels. This allows you to define for your church:

- Which channels are most effective?
- Which channels are least effective?
- Which channels are being underutilized?
- Which channels are being over-utilized?
- Who is leading each of these communication channels?

Once you have your master list of communication channels, you can think through which methods are most effective to communicate each individual message.

Action Step: Where You Will Communicate Your Message

• Make a list of your church-wide communication channels.

• Based on the deliverables you're executing, decide which channels you'll use to deliver your message.

WHEN

When you will communicate your message.

———

Channels				
Channel 1	Channel 2	Channel 3	Channel 4	Channel 5

Timeline

145

After you decide where you'll communicate your message, the next step is to create a timeline.

The purpose of developing the timeline for your communication plan is to help you plan what you're communicating and when you're communicating across each communication channel.

By completing this timeline, you'll walk away with a plan and strategy for how you'll communicate your message to your target audience. This plan and document can be used to proactively get all stakeholders on the same page.

Tips for Planning Your Timeline

1. Start with the end in mind.

Start by mapping out the key information, dates, and milestones that impact your message, and put that on your communication plan template. If there are registration deadlines or other key dates that will impact the communication going out, make note of that on your communication plan.

Then make note of other dates that could impact the communication plan like holidays, school schedules, or other church programs or events.

The message you're communicating is likely not the only thing happening in your church or community. When you have the context of what else is going on, you can plan ahead and make adjustments to your timeline.

2. Decide your start date for communicating your message.

You've nailed down your end dates, so now go back to the beginning to decide when you'll start communicating your message.

How early you start really depends on the context of your message and your target audience. For some big church-wide events (like Christmas or Easter), the start date should be at least four to six weeks out. For some smaller scale messages, you may be fine with two to three weeks.

3. Phase your communication strategy.

There's a marketing term you need to know that has big implications for creating your timeline. It's called "the rule of seven." The rule of seven is the number of impressions it takes before someone new is going to respond to your message.

That's right: Someone needs to hear your message seven times before they respond.

Any message worth communicating is worth communicating more than once.

In today's culture, there is far too much fighting for everyone's time and attention to count on reaching your target audience with one week of communication. You need a prolonged campaign to achieve those seven impressions.

As you map out your start dates, here is some language that can bring clarity to each phase of communication:

Soft launch: These are the first early impressions of your message. The purpose of the soft launch is to build anticipation and awareness for your message with the core of your target audience.

This could mean you're sharing details with your eager target audience, or it could mean you're making basic info available on your website.

Launch: At the launch phase, you're communicating your message when people can hear and respond to your message. That means that it's not too early for the message to feel relevant, but it's timely enough for people to make plans or respond to the message. Typically during the launch phase you're dripping your message across your key communication channels.

Blitz: During the blitz, you're building upon the impressions you've already made of your message and concentrating multiple impressions into a key time when you want people to respond. This typically happens across all your key communication channels to give multiple impressions of your message in a short period of time.

If you're unfamiliar with what this could look like, think about how you see film studios market movies. Months in advance, you may see a movie poster or online teaser trailer designed to start building awareness and ramp up anticipation, especially among hardcore fans. That's the soft launch. Then, a month or so out from the movie release, you may begin to see the trailer on TV and a more consistent presence across communication channels. That's the launch. Then the week before and after the movie is released, the movie is everywhere. The cast is on a press tour, the trailer is playing nonstop, the star's face is plastered on fast food cups. That's the blitz.

Our budgets may look different than film studio budgets (just a bit), but these phased tactics can work for your message too.

4. Decide what you're doing on each box of the template.
You've started at 10,000 feet with mapping out your beginning and end. Now it's time to get down to the ground level for each communication channel you are using.

	Channels				
	Channel 1	Channel 2	Channel 3	Channel 4	Channel 5
Timeline					

For each box in the template, decide what you are doing to communicate for each channel and for each date.

What makes the message communication plan template so helpful is that it forces you to think about each specific channel, on each specific date.

Action Step: When You Will Communicate Your Message

- Work through your communication plan template to decide what you are doing to communicate for each channel and for each date.

HOW

How you will execute your communication plan.

———

At this point you've filled in the communication plan template with:

- What you're doing (deliverables).
- Where you deliver your message (channels).
- When you deliver your message on each channel (timeline).

The last step to developing your communication plan is to figure out how it all happens. You'll do this through creating actionable tasks for each channel and deliverable.

"The result of bad communication is a disconnection between strategy and execution."
-Chuck Martin, former vice president, IBM

Breaking up your communication plan into actionable tasks is vital to effective communication. For any one deliverable to be successful (like a promo video, invite card, stage announcement, or social media post), it will likely require multiple tasks to be completed.

Strategy is hard work. Executing that strategy is just as hard, but equally as essential.

Walk through each item in your communication plan template and break down each aspect into individual, actionable tasks.

Entire books have been written about project management and making things happen. To keep it brief and give you a 10,000-foot-view of what I've learned on executing communication plans, I'll break down four things to include for every task assigned. Those four questions are:

- What is the task?
- Why does this task matter?
- Who's responsible?
- When is it due?

4 Things to Include for Every Task That's Assigned in Your Communication Plan

1. What is the task?
There should be a verb in front of every task.
Write _____.
Design _____.
Coordinate _____.

Be specific about what needs to be completed. Describe any specific notes, context, or background information that would help the person completing the task. Be sure to include any notes about inspiration, tone, or non-negotiables.

2. Why does it matter?

The creative process can be messy. Give each person who is executing each task a clear win.

This win for each task should be tied to something you established in the *Clarify Your Message* section.

Is the win tied to engaging your target audience or overcoming a barrier? Is it tied to something you're trying to accomplish with your message? Include that in the notes for the task.

Some examples of that could be:

- The win for this "Come Sit With Me" invite card is to communicate all the vital information a first-time guest would need to visit our church. This gives each person in our church a simple tool to invite their friends/neighbors/co-workers to come to church and sit with them.
- The win for this stage announcement is to get each person in the service to take a moment right then to sign up online or fill out the registration form in the bulletin. This will help us overcome the barrier of people forgetting to sign up once they leave.

3. Who is responsible?

This seems like a simple idea, but it's often overlooked. Make sure every task has someone who is responsible for completing the task.

My favorite phrase on responsibility comes from the leader who hired me at West Ridge Church, Troy Page, who frequently says, "If you're worried, I'm not." In other words, as long as someone is sweating the details and taking responsibility for making the task happen, then it's all good. Someone should feel the weight and responsibility for each task. Without it, your strategy won't be effective.

4. When is it due?

The communication plan timeline should give you a guide for creating due dates for each task.

Estimate the amount of time each task will take and then work backward from your communication plan to establish clear due dates.

Tip: Project Management Systems

When you need to make sure a project gets completed on time and delegate tasks to the right people, where do you go? There are tons of moving parts involved in communicating a message. So I strongly suggest using some type of project management system. Some of my favorite systems include: Asana, Basecamp, Flow, and Trello.

It doesn't matter if you're a one-person team or part of a sprawling department. Moving a project from idea to completion effectively may take dozens of tasks and involve hundreds of details. If you aren't investing in a project management system to track, centralize, and organize the tasks, you can quickly sink into survival mode and create chaos for you and your team.

Action Step: How You Will Execute Your Communication Plan

• Walk through each item in your communication plan template and break down each aspect of it into individual, actionable tasks.

• For each task, clarify:

  – What is the task?

  – Why does this task matter?

  – Who's responsible?

  – When is it due?

CASE STUDY: ELEPHANT IN THE CHURCH

One of my favorite projects at West Ridge was a series called "Elephant in the Church."

We knew the vast majority of the people who called our church their home church would be there for our Easter services. We wanted to be super intentional about leveraging our Easter services to keep people engaged the week after Easter.

The big idea of the post-Easter series was to address the elephants in the church—to cover the topics everyone thinks about but the church rarely talks about.

Clarity

After clarifying our message and crafting our elevator pitch, our creative team met to brainstorm ideas that would bring the series to life. We knew:

Message	Elephant in the Church
Target Audience	Adults and students
Win: Target Audience	Hear biblical teaching on the hot topics that everyone is thinking about but the church-at-large doesn't talk about.
Win: Church	• Engage people during Easter services and get them to come back. • Teach what God has to say about the hot topics and felt needs of our culture.

Elevator Pitch	"What are the things everyone thinks about but the church rarely talks about? Let's talk about it. Be here throughout the month of April as we cover your top questions and discover what God has to say about the hot topics of our culture."

Creative Brainstorm

Our creative brainstorm focused on creating buzz and anticipation around the series. We brainstormed tons of ideas. But we began to focus our energy around the phrase, "Let's talk about it." We wanted our target audience to actively engage and anticipate what was coming, so that phrase captured the heart of the series and the win for our church.

We focused our creative brainstorm around two different phases of our communication: anticipation and engagement.

Anticipation: How could we get adults and students talking about the series? This was the problem and barrier we had to overcome.

That led us to focus on ideas that could get people in our church and community saying, "What's up with the elephant in the church?"

Engagement: How could we get adults and students interacting with the series? This was the second problem and barrier we had to overcome. It's one thing to build anticipation, but we needed to go a step further.

That led us to an interactive element where people in our church and community could submit the top questions or topics they wanted the series to cover.

Communication Plan

We filtered through the many ideas we came up with during the creative brainstorm and focused on ideas that would work best to build anticipation about the elephant in the church. The deliverables we built our communication plan around consisted of things like:

- Creating a life-sized elephant in the middle of the atrium.
- Placing teaser stickers in random places throughout the church with an elephant and the phrase "Let's talk about it. April 2015."
- Creating teaser videos to play in services and on social media with an elephant walking across the screen and revealing the phrase "Let's talk about it. April 2015."
- Coaching staff to tease the series in their own ministries with intriguing details.

Executing the Plan

Since our planning began more than three months before the series started, we were able to create a phased communication plan to help accomplish the win of our message. Our communication plan template kept everyone on staff on the same page.

	February 22	March 1	March 8	March 15	March 22	March 29	April 3-5
Stage Announcement		• Announcement Video ▫ RUSH Student Camp Registration ▫ Elephant In The Church (Teaser)	• Intro of Sermon ▫ Elephant In the Church – questions submitted ▫ Easter Services - focus on encouraging people to come to Saturday services to make room for first time guests	• Easter Services • Elephant In The Church ▫ Submit questions	• Register For RUSH (Last Week) • Elephant In The Church - Last call for questions submitted • Easter Services	• Easter Services	• Elephant In The Church (PROMO VIDEO)
Print	• Elephant Stickers 5x5 & 3x3 sets • Elephant In The Church Posters in atrium	• Worship Guides (EITC?) • Easter ▫ Postcard ▫ Invites ▫ Waterfall Banner ▫ Outdoor Banner ▫ Easter Posters	• Easter Invite cards available on site • Worship Guides (Easter)	• Easter invite available on site	• Easter invite handed out in service • Easter Worship Guide submitted to printer • East Post Card dropped • Elephant In The Church invites submitted to printer	• Elephant In The Church Worship Guide	• Elephant In The Church posters in atrium
Signage	• Elephant In The Church Posters in atrium	• Easter Posters in atrium • Elephant Stickers ▫ Kid Hallway Windows ▫ Bathroom Mirrors ▫ North/South/East Entrances	• (INSTALLED 3/2-6 • Easter Waterfall Banners in atrium • Easter Roadside Banner • Easter Posters	• Easter Waterfall Banners in atrium • Easter Roadside Banner • Easter Posters	• Easter Waterfall Banners in atrium • Easter Roadside Banner • Easter Posters	• Easter Waterfall Banners in atrium • Easter Roadside Banner • Easter Posters	• REMOVED SUNDAY AFTER 12:45pm service • Easter Waterfall Banners • Easter Roadside Banner
Video		• Video Announcements ▫ Get Connected ▫ Elephant In The Church ▫ RUSH	• RUSH Story	• Easter Promo	• Easter Promo	• Easter Promo	• Elephant In The Church Promo
Social Media Focus Areas	• RUSH Student Camp	• Build intrigue around Elephant In The Church • RUSH Camp	• Easter Service Times • Elephant In The Church Questions • RUSH Story	• Easter Service Times • Elephant In The Church Questions • Easter Promo	• RUSH Registration Ends • Easter Service Times	• Easter Email Blast ▫ Service Times ▫ Promo Video	• Easter Service • Easter Live Pictures • EITC Promo
Web	• RUSH Student Camp (Opens on the 25th) Event Page, Home Page Banner	• RUSH ▫ Home Page • EITC ▫ Homepage Takeover on Sunday?	• Easter At West Ridge ▫ Service Times ▫ Good Friday Square ▫ Baptism Registration	• Easter At West Ridge ▫ Service Times ▫ Good Friday Square ▫ Baptism Registration	• Easter At West Ridge ▫ Service Times ▫ Good Friday Square ▫ Baptism Registration	• Easter At West Ridge ▫ Service Times ▫ Good Friday Square ▫ Baptism Registration ▫ First Time Guest Resources	• Easter At West Ridge ▫ Service Times ▫ First Time Guest Resources • Elephant In The Church ▫ Blog Post

As a bonus, we spent less than $1,000 to pull off our whole communication plan.

Here's what the phases of communication looked like.

6-7 Weeks From Easter: Anticipation

Our win here was to create intrigue for Elephant in the Church. We wanted to get people asking, "What's up with the elephant in the church?"

The ideas we were able to deliver worked like a charm! We built the elephant, placed stickers all over the church, and teased the series through videos and social media posts.

Because our win at this phase of communication was anticipation, when people asked, "What's up with the elephant in the church?", we coached our staff to answer by saying something like, "We're going to talk about it in a few weeks. Come back to hear about the elephant, because you have a crucial role to play!"

For two full weeks we teased the series with the graphics and videos we created and let people know we'd be talking about the elephant in the church a few weeks before Easter.

4-5 Weeks From Easter: Engagement

As we got closer to launching the series, we wanted to shift our strategy from anticipation to engagement. In our services, we shared about the series and invited everyone to go to our website to submit questions or topics they wanted us to cover. We were blown away by the response and the questions we received. By engaging our church in the process, they became invested in the series and were more willing to tell their friends about it.

1-3 Weeks From Easter: Easter Blitz

Once we got closer to Easter, our priority shifted to make Easter the one main message we were communicating. During this time, we were still collecting the Elephant in the Church questions and creating our plan for the topics we would cover during the series.

At Easter Services

We shared a promo video for Elephant in the Church during our Easter services. Following the video, one of our pastors challenged people to come back next week as we explored what the Bible says about the hot topics people had raised.

After completing this series, we reviewed our metrics and goals: We hit our target. Our attendance and first-time guest numbers following Easter were up (compared to the previous year). Beyond that, the series became (and still is to this day) some of the highest viewed and shared messages we've done as a church.

At the end of the day, success for this message wasn't higher attendance or having a good communication plan.

Success was seeing life change within our congregation.
Success was putting Jesus on display through each service.
Success was tackling some of the hardest topics we deal with in our culture and sharing what God has to say about them.
Success was knowing that God can use every plan, every idea, and every moment to draw people to himself.

9

EXECUTE YOUR PLAN

HOW TO PUT YOUR PLAN INTO ACTION.

If you've followed the communication playbook up until this point, you've already clarified your message and developed a plan to communicate your message.

Guess what... you've already completed the hardest part of the communication playbook! But that doesn't mean your work is over.

Now it's time to execute the plan you've developed and communicate your message.

There are three things I want to encourage you to do as you execute your plan.

1. Communicate Internally

The best communication plans can quickly get broken down by a lack of internal communication.

In all my years working in the church, I've never heard staff or leaders complain about too much communication. I've frequently seen issues develop due to a lack of internal communication.

The communication process is messy, fast-moving, and dynamic. As things develop and change, you have to communicate consistently with key stakeholders.

❏ **Have regular check-in meetings.**

Some people think meetings are the bane of their existence, but it's important to have regular meetings to keep your communication plan on track. Do whatever you can to make these meetings quick check-ins that don't drag on. Set a timer, make sure everybody stays focused, and then get back to work—but don't neglect the importance of checking in and making sure everyone is on the same page.

❏ **Use a project management system or internal communication channel.**

We've talked about the importance of a project management system before, but it's crucial that you actually use it. Communication in the church moves fast. As details change, make it part of your routine to keep your projects and tasks up to date.

There are other tools you can use (like Slack or Google Docs) that can keep internal communication centralized. Whatever system you use, find ways to avoid sending an email for every question.

2. Stay Objective in the Creative Process

The creative process is very subjective. It's subjective to the person creating and the person who is experiencing what has been created.

I talk to far too many creatives and communication leaders who filter all their decisions through what their boss or senior pastor would like. That subjective opinion certainly can be a consideration, but it shouldn't be the only filter.

It's always great when your senior pastor likes what you create, but that's not what makes it a win. The win should be that what you create helps you reach your target audience, remove barriers, and accomplish the goal of your message.

❑ **Always go back to objective standards.**
Part of the magic of the three questions we covered in *Clarify Your Message* is that we've established some objectivity in the messiness of the creative process.

Creatives do their best creative work when they have clear boundaries and a clear problem to solve. If they have clarity around the goal, everyone is empowered to screen any strategies or methods through the filter of "will this help us accomplish the goal?"

So as you're executing any creative project, always go back to those objective standards.

❑ **Make senior leaders and managers focus on the objective.**
It's up to you to do the hard work of playing a part in clarifying who you're trying to reach, what you're trying to accomplish, what problems you're trying to solve, and what barriers you're trying to overcome.

Don't let your subjective opinion hold back the creative process.
Don't kill something because you don't like it.
Don't green light something just because you do like it.

Instead, you should be asking:

- Does this help us reach our target audience?
- Does this help us accomplish the win for us and our audience?
- Does this help us overcome communication barriers?

And if you're not the senior leader or manager? You've got a special challenge. You need to help your leadership focus on the objective goals. When you present work, don't just do a quick reveal and wait for their reaction. Set your work up for success by reminding your leadership about the groundwork you did to determine audience, wins, and barriers. Show them your work and explain how it solves those problems.

3. Never Stop Advocating for Your Audience

If I had to sum up the role of a church communication leader, it would be to "identify and remove barriers that are keeping people from taking their next step."

To identify and remove barriers, you must never stop advocating for your audience.

To advocate for your audience, you have to step into their shoes and have empathy for what challenges they may face in responding to your message.

There are a ton of different roles you may play in the communication process. You may be the pastor, ministry leader, or communication leader helping deliver your message to your target audience. Whatever your role is, advocate for that person you're trying to reach in everything you do. Don't just think like a staff member. Identify and remove barriers so you can reach more people with your message.

❏ **As creative pieces are finished, review them with the audience in mind.**
It can be tempting to see the finished work and just be happy it's done. But don't just see it as a proud creative team happy with a job well done. Look at it from the audience's perspective and make sure it's doing what it needs to do.

❏ **Take the audience's side.**
When you have debates or questions about how to solve a creative problem (and you will), always come down on the side of the audience.

Action Step: Execute Your Plan

When you're communicating your message, focus on three things:

- Communicate internally by keeping key stakeholders in the loop.

- Stay objective in the creative process by filtering everything through the three clarifying questions.

- Advocate for your audience by identifying and removing barriers from people taking their next step.

10

EVALUATE YOUR RESULTS

HOW TO EVALUATE YOUR RESULTS THROUGH FOUR QUESTIONS.

The last step of the communication playbook is the most overlooked of them all: evaluation.

I get it. I understand why. Once you're done, there are more things to do, more messages to communicate.

Here's why I would challenge you to rethink what you do after you communicate your message. When you don't pause to evaluate what just happened, you miss out on capturing the most valuable lessons you'll learn about the message you communicate, the way you delivered that message, and the people you're communicating with.

The lessons you can learn in this last step of the communication playbook could unlock the doors to more effective communication the next time around.

At the beginning, you clarified your message through defining your win/target. Now it's time to evaluate:

- Did you hit the target?
- Did you accomplish your win?
- Did you overcome barriers?
- What did you learn about your target audience?

These questions aren't about preferences. This is about moving away from "Did they like this?" and toward "Did this accomplish what we set out to do?"

4 Questions for Evaluating Anything You Do

There are four questions I use every week with our Creative Team at West Ridge. They are basically the questions from "The four helpful lists" by Tom Paterson. These questions are:

What worked?	What did not work?
What was missing?	What was confusing?

1. What worked?

What worked to help you accomplish what you were trying to accomplish? Identify and celebrate the wins. Don't skip this.

Evaluate what worked so you can optimize this for next time.

2. What did not work?

Was there a strategy or method you used that didn't help you hit the target? Did something not get promoted long enough or didn't connect like you were expecting?

Evaluate what did not work so you can fix it next time.

3. What was missing?

Was there something missing within the communication strategy that could have helped remove barriers or made your message more effective? Was the who/what/when/where/how/why communicated with clarity?

Evaluate what was missing so you can add it next time.

4. What was confusing?

In communicating your message, did you identify any disconnections, common questions, or have to clarify anything afterward? Would a first-time guest hearing this message understand what it's all about and why it matters to them?

Evaluate what was confusing so you can clarify it next time.

Building an Evaluation Culture

One of the things I'm most proud of with the creative team I lead at West Ridge Church is the evaluation culture we've built. Every Monday when our team gathers, we evaluate everything that happened in the services the day before along with anything else we're trying to communicate during the week through all of our other communication channels.

When I say everything, I mean everything.

That includes things like text size on announcement slides, transitions in the service, verbiage used in stage announcements, and the people who are communicating from stage.

Because this is a regular rhythm for our team, we get a consistent opportunity to celebrate the wins. No one is caught off guard if we identify something that was not working, missing, or confusing. Most of the time each person on the team is speaking up and owning things that could have been better. Why? Because they were already evaluating if we accomplished our goal.

This evaluation culture has become critical to how we're growing as a team and becoming more effective as a church. You can't build that culture overnight. It takes hard work and leaning into tough conversations with a heart for making things better.

So what culture are you building? Before you jump to the next thing on your list, *pause*. Take a moment individually, or even better with your team, to evaluate what worked, what didn't work, what was missing, and what was confusing.

Action Step: Evaluate Your Results

After you've communicated your message, take some time to evaluate your results by asking these four questions:

• What worked?

• What did not work?

• What was missing?

• What was confusing?

RETHINK

+

REWORK

Ideas to rethink and rework how you
communicate as a church.

Now that we've established the new reality for communication in the church and laid out the communication playbook for delivering your message, it's time to hit some of the other top issues facing the church.

Some of the most dangerous words in the church are "that's how we've always done it."

Our message hasn't changed. However, the ways we deliver our message have changed.

With that in mind, this section is full of ideas and systems to help you rethink and rework communication in your church. While the things we cover here may lead to some big changes, most likely they will lead to some simple things you can rethink and rework that will result in more effective communication.

I encourage you to talk through each of these sections with your team.

MALL KIOSKS

There are two hazards to avoid when you go to the mall:

1. Not getting run over by mall walkers.
2. Avoiding eye contact with the mall kiosk workers.

During a recent trip to the mall, I failed on both counts. I looked down at my phone as I turned the corner and nearly got run over by a swarm of mall walkers. Those folks must have been hitting a record pace, and they certainly weren't going to break their stride for me.

And then there's the beloved mall kiosks. I normally try to avoid eye contact with the kiosk workers at all cost. If they lock eyes with you, you're done. For this trip to the mall, my strategy failed. I needed to get to just one store in the mall, but those eager kiosk workers kept interrupting to spray cologne, offer a Swedish massage, and change my wireless carrier.

I had one very specific purpose for going to the mall, but those overly aggressive kiosk workers kept getting in the way. That's frustrating.

Church or Mall?

Unfortunately this type of experience is not limited to the mall. Something similar happens when I visit churches.

Here's a quick recap of a recent church visit:

- Walking through the church lobby, I passed multiple booths with eager volunteers trying to catch my eye (eerily reminiscent of my trip to the mall).

- An usher handed me a thick bulletin full of announcements as I walked into the service.

- Someone spent 10 minutes in the middle of the service making announcements—basically reading aloud the info already in the bulletin.

- On my way out of the sanctuary, someone handed me another print piece.

- Finally, I had to run the gauntlet of ministry booths again and managed to avoid taking any handouts.

- But one more person was standing at the exit doors with yet another flier.

Everything about my experience that day felt like the church wanted a bunch of things from me, instead of pointing to what God wanted for me. It felt a lot more like walking through the mall instead of the encounter with God I was hoping for.

Too Much Noise

When was the last time you took a thorough look at the experience someone has when they attend your church? Too often we bombard people with bulletins, invite cards, and brochures. Then we fill time in the service telling people about more events and programs. No one wants to feel like they're walking through a mall when they attend your church. They don't want to be sold. They don't want to feel overwhelmed by all the things you want them to sign up for and attend.

Imagine inviting a neighbor who has never attended church before and they experience all that. Would they describe their experience as an encounter with God or something more akin to the mall?

The Proper Posture

The heart behind communicating all these messages to our church is good, because we have a deep desire to see people connect with the church and connect with God. But good intentions aren't enough to connect.

To create engagement, you have to rethink the posture you're communicating from as a church.

What would change in the way you communicate if you shifted your posture and tone from "what we want from people" to "what we want for people?"

As you communicate serving opportunities, are you guilting people into filling a need? Or are you inviting people to serve others as a way of loving God and loving others? Same message, different postures.

As you communicate discipleship opportunities, are you asking people to just sign up and attend? Or are you communicating God's plan and desire for each person to grow in their faith and then providing an opportunity to do just that? Same message, different postures.

As you communicate giving opportunities, are you asking people to just give money to the church? Or are you communicating that as a response to our generous God, we want to give generously to put Jesus on display as a church? Same message, different postures.

The church should be a platform for response to our love for God and others.

Move away from anything that sounds like "We can do it, you can help!" to "You can do it, we can help."

Every time you communicate it's an opportunity to deposit more than you withdraw and add value, with no strings attached.

Rethink the posture of your communication. Move from what we want *from* people, to what we want *for* people.

Discuss

• Take a moment to review the messages you communicated to your church during your last weekend services.

– How many messages were communicated?

– How many were repeated?

– How many were aggressive pitches?

– How many came from a posture of broadcast vs. engagement, sales pitch vs. authentic invitation, church focused vs. audience focused?

• How can your church shift the posture of communication away from what you want *from* people toward what you want *for* people?

URGENT VS. IMPORTANT

In my first three months on the job in church communication, I had to tell a well-intentioned volunteer their ministry was not important. Now I didn't say it like that, but that's exactly what he heard when I couldn't meet his request for a full-fledged marketing campaign for his ministry.

It started like this: I received an urgent email requesting a meeting to talk about a marketing campaign for his ministry. His ministry was dogs. At this church of more than 6,000 people, there was a small handful of dedicated volunteers who took pets to local rehab centers and children's homes to minister to them. It was a really cool ministry—I'm not knocking it.

So I sit down with the volunteer leader and he proceeds to vent his frustrations. He wanted answers for *why* his ministry wasn't being announced on Sunday, *why* his ministry wasn't being featured in the bulletin, *why* their next event wasn't featured on the homepage, and *why* the newsletter he emailed me the *day* before had not been promptly uploaded for the world to see.

Look, I completely understood his frustrations. This ministry was important to him, it made a difference in the lives of others, and he wanted it to be important to everyone else. But in reality, this was a very small, niche ministry best communicated by word of mouth. After looking into it, the ministry web page had a sum total of two visitors over the previous two months. I was one of those visitors, and I was likely sitting across from the other visitor.

Urgent does not always equal important. But it's the urgent requests that keep us from focusing on what's most important.

So here's the tension every communication leader faces: How do I communicate what is important when every ministry wants a marketing campaign?

What do we do when we're stuck between meeting the needs of our audience and meeting the requests of ministry leaders?

Some days it's tempting to give in and let ministry leaders have their way—say yes to every request and crank out the marketing messages. But we'd just be adding to the noise. By trying to make everything important, nothing is important. And in all that noise, the vital message that drives our church would be lost, and we couldn't be effective in helping people take their next step and experience life change.

It's hard work to fight through the clutter and capture what's most important in the midst of everyone's desire to share more and more.

To manage this tension, I challenge you to rethink the idea of fairness in church communication.

Fairness should not be a value in church communication.

Not all events, ministries, or programs are created equal.
Not all announcements need to be made from the stage.
Not every ministry warrants a menu listing on your website.

Like my friend Tony Morgan says, "When fairness drives your communication strategy, your least important message has the same weight as your most important message." If you try to treat every event or program the same and make everything important, nothing is important.

The urgent things you deal with are rarely the most important. The only person who can fix that is you.

Discuss

- Do you spend more time on the urgent or the important?

- What are some ways you can focus less on the urgent and more on the important?

- What are some ways to give those urgent items an outlet so they're still communicated but they don't crowd out the important? Could you use a separate Facebook group, targeted email list, or equip the ministry with some print and digital resources?

A SIMPLE SOLUTION
TO MESSAGE OVERLOAD

The top challenge most churches face is coincidentally the same challenge your audience is facing: message overload.

Every week of the year, churches have messages that need to be communicated to the congregation and community. The barrier that keeps us from effectively communicating those messages is limited bandwidth (that also keeps our audience from effectively hearing messages).

There's a limit to the number of messages your church can effectively communicate each week. Plus, your audience is already processing 10,000 branded messages each day, so there's a limit to how many messages they can handle.

Most churches are trying to communicate too many messages each week. Our services, bulletins, and social media posts are crammed full with so many messages that it's not only overwhelming for us to create, it's also overwhelming for our audience to absorb.

So what do you do when you have too many messages to communicate in your church?

There's one thing your church can do to bring clarity to this chaos of communication. It's as simple as answering this question for each week of the year:

What are the one to two things you want everyone in your church to know this week?

Why Only One to Two Messages?

This is the sweet spot for effective communication.

Good communication doesn't come easy, and it takes time to do it effectively. When you only have one or two messages, you can focus all your energy on communicating those messages really well. With every message you add, it becomes exponentially more difficult to communicate each message with any effectiveness.

One or two messages is also the sweet spot for what your audience can hear and remember. When you announce five or six (or more) things on a Sunday morning, your audience just gets overwhelmed.

What's it going to take for you to filter all your messages down to one to two for each week?

Create Standards

If you're going to limit the number of messages you share each week, the first step has to be creating standards for what you communicate. And if you only share one or two messages, they need to apply as broadly as possible. So what qualifies as a church-wide message?

These are the standards I use as a filter to see if a message should be communicated church-wide:

- ✓ Does it impact 80% of our audience?
- ✓ Is it a direct next step that would add value to our audience?
- ✓ Is it a key on-ramp to a ministry?

Church-wide communication gets priority for stage announcements, home page features, video promos, postcards, and social media posts.

There are times when we have one to two church-wide events going on during a week, and other times when we don't have anything that has to be communicated. If that happens in your church, you have permission to *not* do a stage announcement that day. I promise, life will go on.

On a lower tier than church-wide events, we have niche ministry events that don't fit those standards. These are communicated primarily through things like social media, announcement slides, and the event listings on our website. These types of messages are promoted heavily at their own ministry gatherings where it does apply to 80% of their audience. For example, a kids' movie night could be promoted heavily to kids and parents in the kids' ministry newsletter and kids' worship service, but not from the stage during the main worship service.

At the end of the day, here's the goal I have for our audience: I want anyone connected to our church to know the one to two things that are most important right now.

Sometimes that's an event coming up, a teaching series we're starting, or a takeaway from a message we want them to be talking about. This may sound harsh, but if it's not part of the one to two things that are most important for our audience, then it's likely not going to be featured in our service or featured in our main communication channels.

Church-Wide Communication Grid

Limiting the number of messages you share each week requires careful planning. As communication leaders, it's critical we have a way to see the big picture: what's being communicated, when are we communicating it, and what channels are we using. This big picture perspective of what you're communicating each week is essential to identifying bandwidth issues for your team and your church.

To plan out these messages, I developed a church-wide communication grid. It gives us an overview of what we're communicating each week of the year and has been a game changer. We use a shared Google Doc, which gives our whole team one centralized place to see what's happening.

Here's what our planning document looks like:

2016	SERIES	TOPIC	SPEAKER	MC	CALENDAR	NEXT STEPS	VIDEO	SERVICE NOTES
Jul 22	Elephant In The Church	Parenting	Paul			Promotion Sunday	Roundtable Teaching Video	
Jul 29	Elephant In The Church	How do we love those who aren't like us	Brian	Paul	7/29 - Teacher Appreciation Sunday? / 8/1 - First Day of School (Paulding & Cobb)	Annual Report Celebration? / Promotion Sunday / Student Ministry Kickoff	Promotion Sunday	
Aug 5	Rethink Prayer	Coming into His presence	Brian	Paul	8/5 - Teacher Appreciation Sunday? / 8/5 - Promotion Sunday / 8/7 - Middle School Kickoff / 8/8 - High School Kickoff / 8/9-10 - Global Leadership Summit	Student Ministry Kickoff / Group Launch / Night of Worship / Album Release		Unique Get Connected Card?
Aug 12	Rethink Prayer	Purpose of Prayer	Paul	Terence		Group Launch	ReEngage Story	Unique Get Connected Card?
Aug 19	Rethink Prayer	Being in Alignment with God's will	Brian	Steve	Group Launch / 8/23 - YA Gathering / 8/24 - Women's Event / 8/25 - Men's Event	Group Launch		Communion
Aug 26	Rethink Prayer	Praying with Christ's Authority	Brian	Paul	Group Launch / 8/26 - Married Groups Event / 8/26 - Singles Gathering / 8/27 - ReEngage	Group Launch Reminder / Night of Worship / Album Release		
Sep 2	Rethink Prayer	Praying Scripture	Paul	Jason	9/3 - Labor Day	Night of Worship / Album Release		Baptism
Sep 9	Celebrating 21 Years	21 Year Anniversary	Brian Paul Terence	Paul	9/9 - 21 Year Anniversary / 9/9 - Night of Worship / Album Release	Annual Report / Night of Worship / Album Release	Vision Fund	Small Group Commissioning
Sep 16	Stand-Alone	Reaching Scotland	Robert Bell Church Planter from Scotland	Kevin Ruth	9/16 - Brian and Paul out in Burkina	Next Steps Push for 4 weeks in October	Vision Fund	Communion

This communication grid gives us a single, shared space to plan each week of the year:

- What teaching series are we in?
- What topic are we teaching about?
- What are the one to two next steps we're communicating?
- What's on the calendar that will impact communication? (That could include other events in the church, holidays, or the calendar for local schools.)
- How are we using each key communication channel (physical and digital) to communicate our one to two messages?

You can download and customize the church-wide communication grid here: RethinkCommunicationBook.com/resources

It doesn't matter what this document looks like for you. Use the free grid if you want, but find your own solution, use your own specific channels, make it your own. What's important is that you have a way to see big picture what you're communicating each week and make adjustments when necessary. This has helped me countless times to identify when we have too much we're trying to communicate during a service and gives me the time to make changes.

———

As we've put our energy and focus into capturing those one to two things each week, we've seen the response and engagement sky-rocket.

What are the one to two things you want everyone in your church to know this week?

Create standards that you filter each message through.
Map out your messages through a communication grid.
See how communicating fewer things better is more effective.

It won't come easy, but it's worth it.

LESS IS MORE

I have a love/hate relationship with the Cheesecake Factory.

I love the cheesecake. I hate the menu.

The last time I went to the Cheesecake Factory, it took a solid 15 minutes to look through all the different options. They have over 250 items on their menu, 85 of which are different chicken dishes! Come to think of it, maybe all this menu indecision is why there's always an hour-long wait to get a table.

I have no doubt that all the food is good, but I'm overwhelmed every time I look at the menu. I always end up asking the wait staff for their recommendation.

The Opposite Menu

While my experience at Cheesecake Factory is overwhelming, let me tell you about my first visit to In-n-Out. Not only was this a heavenly burger experience, it was also stress-free.

In-n-Out made my process simple. Instead of hundreds of options, their menu had four items: burgers, fries, drinks, milkshakes. In a brief moment, I could read the whole menu and make my selection.

Here are a few insights about how they run their operation:

- They know what makes them unique.
- They are able to do more with less.
- They know what they do best.
- They put their resources behind making what they do better.
- They remove barriers from the process of getting food by keeping things simple and excellent.

Cheesecake Factory Church or In-n-Out Church

If your church was a restaurant, which one would you be?

Most churches are providing a Cheesecake Factory menu, and it's overwhelming people. Lost in all of the programs, events, and ways to connect is a clear path for how people can take the next step in their walk with God.

Churches need to simplify.

We just covered reducing the number of messages you share in the *A Simple Solution to Message Overload* section. But you also need to reduce the number of next steps you offer.

Case Study: Get Connected Card

At West Ridge Church, we've worked diligently to simplify our menu. We learned the hard way that giving too many options dramatically lowers engagement.

As a church, we have a few core next steps we want to keep in front of people every week: salvation, baptism, membership class, small groups, serving, and missions.

That's a lot of steps right there. So we simplify it to a single step: Filling out our Get Connected Card.

We ask people to provide their contact information and indicate if there's a next step they're interested in taking (from the list above). We also give people a link so they can fill out the card online if they prefer.

Instead of explaining all those options every single week, we communicate the simple idea of taking a next step, whatever that may be.

It often sounds something like this: "Whether this is your first time here or you've been coming here for awhile, we'd love to connect with you and help you take your next step in following Jesus. Whether that's getting in a group, serving on a team, or learning more about our church, you can take your next step by filling out the Get Connected

Card you received on the way in. You can also fill out that same card on our app or website. Once we receive it, someone from our team will be in touch with you within 24 to 48 hours. We can't wait to connect with you!"

By reducing all the possible next steps down to a single step of filling out the Get Connected Card, we've seen a massive jump in engagement.

Discuss

- Does your menu look more like the one from the Cheesecake Factory or In-n-Out?

- Are there next steps or messages you're communicating that may be overwhelming people with too many options?

- What are some ways you could do more with less and simplify your message?

QUIT DOING ANNOUNCEMENTS

Have you ever walked out of a church service and overheard someone saying, "Wow, those announcements were so powerful today!"

The very mention of the word "announcements" brings back memories of being stuck in a pew, listening to someone read the bulletin for 10 minutes about everything on the church calendar that week.

Look, let me be clear. I'm not saying you should never talk about your upcoming events during your service. What I am saying is we have to tip over this sacred cow of taking 10 minutes in every service to read all the different things happening in the church.

Churches should not assume if it's announced from the stage, it's remembered in the seats.

The challenge churches face is that we have life-changing opportunities for people to take advantage of, but they are often getting tuned out, ignored, or forgotten during the typical announcement time.

That means we have to rethink how we handle announcements.

If this is a struggle for your church, here are some practical announcement tips to get you started.

Quit Doing Announcements, Start Doing Next Steps

The best announcements don't feel like announcements. They feel like a natural next step to what people have just experienced.

What's the difference between an "announcement" and a "next step"? Announcements are information rich and inspiration poor. Next steps offer a relevant, clear, and compelling call to action for your audience to respond to.

Create Standards for What's Announced

Your congregation is looking to you to help them decide what they need to know. But if you treat everything as important, nothing will be important.

Communication standards may look different at every church, but it's critical to have consistent standards for deciding what will get stage time and what will not. If you need a starting point, I'd suggest going back to what I covered in the *A Simple Solution to Message Overload* section. Using those standards will remove a lot of the noise that drowns out the most important next steps you offer as a church.

Don't Just Read the Bulletin: Share Your Elevator Pitch

If a message is worth sharing, it's worth taking the time to clarify. You've got a brief moment to deliver your message and invite people to respond to it. Everything you do during that brief moment of communication matters.

As I mentioned earlier, you should create an elevator pitch for any message you communicate. Working through this exercise helps you clarify how you can communicate your message so it grabs the attention of your audience and sparks a response.

Get Creative With Your Methods

Don't get stuck in a rut with how you communicate your next steps. If you're sharing your next steps in the same place, at the same time, in the same ways each week, your audience is likely already tuning them out.

Once you decide what you need to share from the stage, creatively think through what method would be most effective for communicating that next step. Here are some methods you can add to your toolbox that aren't the standard talking head on stage:

- **Video:** If you have more than a few next steps or if you're sharing something that people need to see to fully understand and connect with, announcement videos are a great solution!

- **Mention:** Can it be shared in 15 seconds or less? Is it something that connects to another moment already in the service? Make it a quick mention with a clear call to action. For example, if you're baptizing people in the service, take a quick moment to mention the next opportunity to be baptized. Tell people when it is and what their next step would be. It doesn't have to take a minute of talking about something for it to be effective.

- **Share a story:** Do you have a compelling story of someone in your church who was impacted by a next step you're sharing? Consider using a video testimony of their story. A personal story of a changed life will have a much greater impact than a few talking points.

- **Point people to a communication hub:** Do you have a few consistent next steps you want to communicate weekly? Things like baptism, volunteering, small groups, or membership? Point them to a consistent communication hub where they can take their next step in any of those areas. That may mean pointing people to your connection card or information desk. If you do this consistently, you build an expectation that people can always go to your communication hub to take their next step.

Quit doing announcements and help someone take their next step today.

Discuss

- How effective are your announcements?

- What would change in your church if you skipped the announcements one week? Anything?

- What's one way you can take this week's announcements and make just one of them more compelling and engaging?

7 REASONS WHY YOU'RE NOT GETTING A STAGE ANNOUNCEMENT

The last section talked about quitting announcements. OK, so it's not actually *quitting* announcements, but instead giving intentional next steps instead of just blasting information. That's good progress. However, there are still ministries and leaders asking to have their thing announced from stage.

Managing stage announcements can be one of the most challenging things in service planning for pastors and communication leaders. Without a system and strategy in place, you can quickly find yourself stuck in a rhythm of spending 10 minutes on announcements at the end of the service, while not being effective with any of them.

Time is limited and stage announcements are not the answer to everything.

Here are seven reasons why you're not getting a stage announcement:

1. It doesn't apply to at least 80% of the audience.
This is the most important question you can ask when deciding if something should be announced from stage. To capture and keep the attention of your audience, the announcements should apply to the vast majority of the people hearing them. This will help filter many of the things that may be getting announced at your church, and allow you to focus on key church-wide messages.

There may be times when you break from this rule to communicate key ministry on-ramp events, foundational ministries, or when it's a direct next step for what's being preached about in the sermon.

As an example, we don't announce every student ministry event from the stage. However, when our summer camp comes around each year, we announce that for three to four weeks because it's a crucial on-ramp opportunity for students. We know that if we can get students engaged in that summer camp, they will become engaged throughout the rest of the year.

We may also include announcements that don't apply to 80% of the audience but do help people take a next step in that week's sermon topic. You may not announce all the care and support ministries you have as a church each week. However, if you're teaching about addiction during a service, it's a great opportunity to announce your church's ministries and resources for those who want to take a next step in dealing with addiction.

2. It should be announced at your ministry event, not the whole church.

For example, if you need to communicate an event happening with student ministry, the most effective place to get the word out is at your student ministry gatherings. Same applies to other areas.

3. There's no clear "why."

If you can't share the "why" associated with the announcement in less than 30 seconds, it's going to be hard to communicate effectively from stage. It's going to be even harder to get your audience to care.

4. The announcement sends them on a rabbit trail.

Is there childcare? Where is the event? Is registration required? Without knowing the who, what, when, where, how, and why of the announcement, you'll quickly create more questions than answers and lose your audience in the process. Effective announcements have a clear next step involved for what they should do next. It's OK to not mention every detail, but it's crucial to communicate where they can find all the information they need. For us at West Ridge, we always communicate that they can get more information at our Help Center in the atrium or at WestRidge.com. If it's announced on a Sunday, we feature that message on the home page of our website so it's easy to find for our visitors.

5. It's not an effective time to announce it.

Timing is everything. One of the keys to developing a communication plan is to be strategic about when you're going to promote programs and events. Don't waste bandwidth announcing something before your audience can do anything with that information.

For example, if you're announcing Christmas service times, it's more important to announce that in the three to four weeks before Christmas when your audience is making plans than it is in November when it's likely too far off to do anything with that information.

6. It's a bandage for a short-term problem, not an on-going strategy.
Do you need two more volunteers in the nursery? There are two ways you can approach this:

> Option #1: Announce from stage that you need two more volunteers in the nursery. You'll likely find the volunteers, but you'll create a precedent for every ministry to ask for stage announcements anytime they are a couple volunteers short. Also, your audience will think the only place you need volunteers is in the nursery.

> Option #2: You strategically and consistently announce to the whole audience that there are opportunities across the church to serve and make an impact. This way you're encouraging everyone to take their next step in serving and building your volunteer base across all ministries.

7. There are too many things being announced already.
If you really want your announcements to be effective, pick one to two announcements that are the most important for your audience to know and say no to the rest.

SOCIAL MEDIA PLAYBOOK

It's easy to start a social media account for your church.
It's far more challenging to actually be effective on social media.

Gone are the days of debating whether or not churches should be using social media. According to Pew Research Center[7], nearly two-thirds of all adults are active on social media. If we're going to be effective as the church in reaching our culture today, it's critical for us to take a serious look at how we can utilize social media for ministry.

Through my years in ministry as a communication and creative leader, I've talked to a lot of pastors and church leaders about social media. The interesting thing I've found is that they all seem to experience the same challenges and frustrations.

Almost every church I talk to is unsure of their strategy, overwhelmed at trying to keep up with posting, and frustrated that they're not getting more engagement.

So how do we fix that? It starts with building a solid foundation and a social media communication plan.

Social Media Playbook

❏ **Step 1: Start with why.**

It's easy to start a social media presence these days without ever defining what the purpose and strategy is behind it.

Why are you using social media in the first place? What are you hoping to accomplish? What's your strategy to help get you there?

If you're doing it just because everyone else is doing it, or you're just looking for a new place to post your bulletin announcements, don't waste your time.

For us at West Ridge Church, our social media strategy is to inform, engage, and encourage our audience. What does that practically look like for us?

Inform

We inform our audience through sharing next steps and opportunities that would add value to their lives. We share stories of people who have been impacted by what we offer at the church and give people a clear call to action for how they can take their next step.

Engage

We engage our audience through building community and conversation. Social media is more like tennis than bowling. It's about two-way interactions through listening and engaging with our audience. As a church, we're intentional about sharing stories, humor, and prayer requests that foster conversation and engagement.

Engagement doesn't end with the content you post. It starts there and provides a platform to engage with anyone who is taking the bold step to engage with you on social media.

Encourage

We encourage and resource our audience through helpful content, Scripture, resources, inspiring quotes, and challenges for the day. There's a very real possibility that what we share may be one of the few positive posts they see all day in their feeds. That's an opportunity for us to share hope, love, and encouragement.

❏ Step 2: Establish your social media platforms.

Facebook? Twitter? Instagram? Snapchat? Pinterest? The options are endless, and it can be difficult to know where to start. Before you create a bunch of accounts, here are a few things to consider. What platforms are actively being used in your congregation? What platforms are being used in your community or the demographic you're trying to reach? The answer to those questions can make all the difference in deciding where to start.

Once you have your list, you have to identify what your bandwidth looks like as a whole for being able to post, monitor, and respond on each of the platforms you've chosen. Remember, slow and steady trumps fast and unsustainable. Focus on building a solid presence your audience can rely on.

❏ Step 3: Define your target audience.

Who is our audience? What do they value? What type of content are they looking for on each platform?

As church communication leaders, we have to think like our audience, not staff members. Staff is looking for promotion and awareness. Our audience desires relationship, value, and engagement.

This is the kryptonite for most church social media accounts. The vast majority of churches get their start in social media with a "what's in it for me" mentality. Every post seems to be asking people to sign up, show up, or share.

To be successful with social media, you have to deposit more than you withdraw and share content that will add value to your audience. Take the time to define the audience you're trying to reach. This step will help you become an advocate through what you share.

❑ **Step 4: Outline the content you want to share.**
The content you share should be an overflow from your strategy. As you work through your strategy, identify the types of content and sources you can utilize.

If you ever find yourself stuck on what you could be posting, here are some practical ideas to get you started:

Inform
- Events and programs
- First-time guest resources
- Tease the topic or service for that week

- Key next steps you're announcing in service
- Volunteer opportunities
- Generosity initiatives
- Small group/Sunday school opportunities
- Baptism
- Membership
- Teaching series

Engage

- Questions around the sermon topic
- Stories of life change
- Ask for prayer requests
- Behind the scenes
- Photos from events/services
- Respond to current events and trending topics
- Video content from services
- Set list of worship songs used in services

Encourage

- Bible verses
- Repost audio/video from sermon
- Inspiring quotes
- Challenge for the day
- Helpful articles/books
- Memorable quotes from sermons

These are all just broad ideas. How you bring these ideas to life is by infusing them with your unique story and voice as a church.

❏ **Step 5: Create a communication schedule.**
Now that you have ideas and content sources in place, the next step is to build a communication schedule.

The best place to start is by establishing a weekly rhythm for each of your platforms. Once you decide on the platforms, number of posts per day, and the type of content you want to share every week, you can build a weekly rhythm for your social media communication plan.

Having a weekly rhythm in place takes much of the guess work out of what you should be posting. It gives you a starting point. Now you can fill in the gaps with other content that would be timely or engaging to your audience.

❏ **Step 6: Assemble your toolbox.**
There are hundreds of tools you can utilize to help you create engaging content on social media. Here are a few of my favorites:

Social Media Scheduling and Monitoring
- SproutSocial.com
- HootSuite.com
- BufferApp.com

Design Tools
- Web: Canva.com, DesignFeed.io
- Software: Adobe Photoshop, Pixelmator
- Photos: Unsplash.com, PixaBay.com, RocketRepublic.com, Pexels.com
- Graphics: GraceWayMedia.com, CreativeMarket.com, GraphicRiver.net

Where do I go from here?
Social media is hard work, but it's worth it.

Don't be afraid to fail.

Start somewhere.

While it's good to engage with your audience, avoid getting sucked into the social stream.

Try new things, take risks, and don't forget it's about relationships, not follower count.

7-DAY SOCIAL MEDIA PLAYBOOK FOR PASTORS

———

Pastors, what could happen if you spent a few minutes a day creating conversations and connections through social media? Here's a play-by-play guide.

If there was an opportunity to expand your ministry reach and connect with your church and community where they are during the week, would you take it? There's an opportunity in front of you ripe with ministry potential. That opportunity is social media.

You have all the tools you need to reach more people than ever before. You just need to learn how to use these tools to expand your ministry reach. All it will take from you is investing a few minutes a day. I promise, the return will be worth it.

To help you get started, here is a seven-day playbook to walk you through what this could look like. Adjust however you'd like to fit your style, community, and culture.

Day 1: Monday

❑ **Ask "How can I pray for you?"**

Start off the week by connecting with people and asking how you can pray for them. If you have an experience you can briefly share that demonstrates the power of prayer in your life, share it! This is such an easy way to connect with people and hear the burdens they're experiencing. As people comment, make sure to reply with a word of encouragement or simply let them know you're praying for them.

Day 2: Tuesday

❑ **Celebrate a win that's happening in your church.**

Looking back at the last few weeks at your church, what's a win you can celebrate? You could share a photo and story of someone who was recently baptized or who gave their life to Christ. This could be a ministry experiencing growth and seeing lives changed. Think about some wins the average person in your church may not know about, and use this as an opportunity to share them.

Day 3: Wednesday

❑ **Share what God is teaching you.**

Through this season in your life, what is God teaching you? Where have you seen God at work in your life recently? Share this from your heart, and end the post with a question that may spark some engagement by saying "What is God teaching you right now?" Get real and vulnerable. This is a great way to humanize yourself for people who only see you on a stage behind a pulpit.

Day 4: Thursday

❑ **Go behind the scenes of your message.**

People love getting a behind-the-scenes look at something they're going to experience. So offer some text or even a video about what you're sharing in your upcoming message. If there's a key question or felt need you're going to be addressing, share that! It's a great way to build anticipation for your sermon. There may even be an opportunity to get feedback or stories about a topic you're going to share. Ask for that feedback and see if you can work those examples into your message this week.

Day 5: Friday

❑ **Honor a volunteer.**

Is there an unsung hero at your church? Someone who faithfully serves behind the scenes, but may never get the credit they deserve? Snap a photo of them during the week and honor them through a post. This will be a huge encouragement to that volunteer, but will also be an opportunity to demonstrate how important volunteers are to your church.

Day 6: Saturday

❑ **Invite people to church.**

Why are you excited about church tomorrow? Share that and invite people to join you. Yes, you should share your service times and maybe a web link to get directions to your church. But that's not the only thing you should share. Here's the key: Don't make this just about the information. Make this about the why. As you write this post, think of the person who may be on the fence about coming to church tomorrow. Share the why, not just the what, and encourage people to bring someone with them. This is also another opportunity to share about the topic of this week's sermon.

Day 7: Sunday

❏ **Facebook or Instagram live after your message.**

Take a few minutes after your services to jump on Facebook or Instagram Live to dive deeper into the application of your message that day. Share a brief recap of what you talked about in the message for the people who are watching on social media and weren't at church that day. Then take a moment to encourage people with how they can apply what they heard in the message. If there was a story or Scripture you didn't have time to share during the service, take a moment to share it here. This is one of the best opportunities for pastors to connect with people on social media right now.

Frequently Asked Questions

How long should I spend creating these posts?

I'd suggest blocking off 10 to 15 minutes a day to invest in this. Just remember, your job isn't done after you hit "post." Social media is a two-way conversation, not a one-way bullhorn. Make sure to take a few moments during the day to engage with any comments that come in.

How can I improve engagement?

Make these posts as visually engaging as you can. Use photos to bring them to life or a simple graphic to drive home the message. There are some free resources out there for photos such as Pexels.com, Unsplash.com, or PixaBay.com. For graphics, you could use Canva.com or a similar application.

What social platforms should I use?
Facebook is where I'd start. Instagram would be next.

Is there a way to plan ahead?
Yes! You can schedule content on Facebook through third-party services such as HootSuite.com and Buffer.com. There are even ways you can schedule content on Instagram through an application such as SkedSocial.com. Scheduling can be a great way to block off some extra time to write several posts at once and then post them automatically. However, you can't automate engagement. Engagement is manual. If you schedule your posts, make sure you're carving out the time to engage with the people who are engaging with you.

After I do the seven-day experiment, what's next?
This seven-day experiment is designed to get you started and show you the ministry impact social media can have. Don't feel the pressure to post every day, but I would encourage you to be consistent in using social media to connect with your church and community.

———

What's going to happen through this seven-day social media experiment? God only knows. You'll never know until you give it a try.

YOU'VE GOT
ONE JOB

In my first role as a communication director in the church, I came in with passion and drive to do three years worth of projects in the first three months. What followed was a season of ministry where I was completely overwhelmed and on the road to early burnout.

Every day I was getting requests from ministries about promoting their events or fulfilling some type of communication need. As these communication requests came in, my instinct was always to say yes. Why? I wanted to see their event or ministry be successful. However, if I'm honest, there was a little more to it than that.

What I've had to learn the hard way is that my tendency to say yes often comes from a fear of being disliked. I fear people won't understand that an answer of "no" doesn't mean I don't support them or what they do. I fear they will make personal judgements about me instead of understanding the role I play as a communication leader. I fear they will talk behind my back and blame me for their event's lack of success.

It turns out, if you make communication and leadership decisions based on being liked, you're going to be ineffective.

That's exactly what happened to me. Trying to make everyone happy was burning me out. I was making decisions through a "survival mode" mentality, just trying to make it through each busy season. I should have been leading us toward the best communication practices and better results for our church.

My One Job

It took a light bulb moment for me to realize I had one job.

I walked into our empty worship center looking for clarity. I knew I couldn't make everyone happy, and I knew that something needed to change. I had a real honest moment with God, just asking the question, "What's my one job?"

I found my eyes moving from focusing on the stage to focusing on the seats. It hit me, that at the core of what I do, I needed to focus on being an advocate for the person in the seat. I needed to stop being crippled by the fear of being disliked, and start focusing on being an advocate for each person we communicate with.

That moment changed everything for me.

Become an Advocate for Your Audience

When you're on staff, it's easy to just think like a staff member.

When you're thinking like a staff member, you end up:

- Creating barriers and complexities that can confuse your audience.
- Thinking like an insider and becoming numb to the things that can confuse your audience and make it hard for them to connect.
- Overwhelming your audience by promoting too many things, because the win for you is just getting the information out there for the staff.

When you're an advocate for your audience, you focus on:

- Identifying and removing barriers from people taking their next step.
- Building communication standards so you're helping your audience know what's most important.
- Managing communication bandwidth so you're not overwhelming people with too much information or too much promotion.

I had to realize that the win for me is not making the staff happy. The win is that I am an advocate for the people we are communicating with.

Don't let the fear of being disliked cripple you from being effective in the ministry God has called you to.

There are a ton of different roles you play as a communication leader. You may write, design, edit, or shoot. But at the end of the day, make sure you don't forget the foundation of what you're doing as a communication leader.

Advocate for the person you're communicating with as a church. Advocate for that person you're praying for in your neighborhood or community who might come to church for the first time this week. Advocate for your audience.

Discuss

- What does making other ministries happy accomplish if it's harming your overall communication ministry?

- Are there ways your church advocates for pastors, leadership, staff, or longtime members instead of the wider congregation or first-time guests?

- How can you communicate a "no" to ministries but still give them helpful options?

REDEFINING EXCELLENCE

For far too long, I was obsessed with the concept of excellence. I always felt excellence was a value often forgotten or overlooked in the church world, and I tried to make it my mantra as a young creative to raise anything I could up to a level of excellence I could be proud of.

I still love and value excellence. I think it's critical to effectively communicating the story of what God is doing in and through our churches.

Without even realizing it, my definition of excellence became equated to perfection, and perfection was never in reach.

As I look back at that first season of ministry, there was something missing. My focus for achieving excellence created a steady rhythm of being overwhelmed, frustrated, and feeling like I never arrived anywhere. Everywhere I looked, I found things that needed fixing, and I faced challenges with limited resources and staff. I wasted sideways energy on so many things I couldn't control, feeling like excellence was a destination I'd never actually get to.

If I was going to survive and be effective in the call God placed on my life, a couple things needed to change.

Redefine Excellence

I had to learn that you can't measure excellence by what another church is doing. Comparing what your church does with another church that has a larger team or bigger budget is a waste of time.

Excellence cannot be a comparison game. It can't be, otherwise excellence would be out of reach for many of us. You can still pursue excellence regardless of the size of your team or budget, but it will require you to focus your attention on the right things.

Excellence isn't perfection. Excellence isn't a destination. Excellence is doing the best with what you have.

Excellence is about the expectation and mindset that you are going to maximize the team, tools, and resources God has given you.

That should free all of us up to let go of the things we cannot control, and focus on making the most of what God has given your church.

Embrace Stewardship

As leaders in the church, we constantly encounter things that aren't as good as we think they should be and need fixing. Some of these things are within our realm of control to fix. Others are not.

God has not called us to fix everything we see. Instead, God has called us to be good stewards of the time, talent, resources, and responsibilities he's placed in our hands. Our role is not just a job. It's a stewardship.

If God hasn't placed a role, decision, or project in your hands, that's OK! Dive into the things that are your responsibility, and be a good steward of them. Let go of the things you can't control. Stop worrying about them.

What I've learned from this concept (and Matthew 25:14-30), is that if you can be a good steward of what God gives you, he promises to give you more.

Working in the church is a grind.
It's a challenge that few understand.
Don't give up.
Take it one day at a time, and be a good steward of everything God gives you.

At the end of the day, I think that's what excellence truly is.

Discuss

- How do you define excellence?

- What would change for you, your ministry, and your church if you stopped chasing excellence and focused on stewardship?

4 QUESTIONS EVERY GREAT STORY ANSWERS

Many years ago, before I was a creative arts pastor, I got my start in creative ministry as "the video guy." At the time, that meant I mostly created highlight videos from camps or mission trips. Honestly, it didn't take a whole lot of skill to do what I was doing. I would just film moments happening on the trips, edit out the bad stuff, keep the good stuff, throw in some music, and call it a day.

One time the pastor I was working with asked for help making testimony videos. As the video guy, this was my role. However, there was one small issue... I knew how to hit record, make things look decent in the camera, and make highlight videos. I didn't have the first clue how to tell a story.

Nobody ever taught me anything about that. No one taught me what makes some stories memorable and other stories forgettable.

What I had to learn and discover the hard way is that effective storytelling isn't as simple as hitting the record button. It's more than just picking out the right camera or buying the right editing software. It's about tapping into the power of storytelling.

It took me a while to learn that the effectiveness of your video is far more dependent on how you're crafting the story than it is on what equipment you use or budget you have. If it was all about the budget and equipment, you would think films like *Battleship* with its estimated $220 million budget would have been the best movie of the year. But it turns out, if the story isn't compelling, it doesn't matter how great the equipment or budget is.

Stories play a crucial role in our churches today, just as they have since the beginning of church. It was Jesus' chosen method of teaching as we see in Scripture with his parables.

If we can become better storytellers—whether through video, written copy, social media, or other mediums—we'll have an opportunity to communicate more effectively for our churches.

What Is a Story?

I define story as "the journey and response of a character facing a conflict."

Sometimes, the character is a person. That story may sound like a man, whose life was falling apart with drug and alcohol abuse, taking a bold step to keep his life and family together.

There are times where the "character" may be your church. As an example, our church is adopting a new village in Guatemala. That story would look like the journey of our church transforming a village in Guatemala that is mired in poverty and lacks clean water.

Other times the "character" is broad and the goal is that the audience puts themselves in the story as the protagonist. For example, that may look like a person who thinks they have nothing to offer God but still has the opportunity to serve and use their gifts.

Every story is different. But at the end of the day, stories tell the journey and response of a character facing conflict.

Now that we have the concept of what a story is, there are four specific questions I believe every effective story answers.

Question #1: What Is the Conflict?

What's the conflict or problem the character is trying to solve?

Conflict is simply the struggle between two opposing forces. That might be an internal conflict or an external conflict.

Without conflict, you don't have a story worth telling. Think about what kind of story *Star Wars* would be if Luke Skywalker never dealt with his past and never faced Darth Vader. Think about what kind of story *Shawshank Redemption* would be if Andy Dufresne never ended up in jail for crimes he didn't commit.

Conflict shapes who we are as people and is the key to relating to our audience.

When your story sounds too good to be true, it's too hard to relate to.

As you identify the story you want to tell, first identify the conflict in the story.

Question #2: What Is the Solution?

For the internal or external conflict in the story, what was or what could be the solution? What's going to fix the problem the character is facing?

Here's the cool thing: We serve a God who is in the solution business. We have the Bible that lays out the very Word of God, which provides a path for us. In the stories we share, we can point to Jesus as the solution.

This was groundbreaking for me, because it changed what I looked for in the type of stories we were sharing as a church. Instead of just focusing on the most sensational stories, I began searching for the simple but relatable stories of people who were facing a conflict and found a solution in something we had to offer as a church.

After you identify the conflict in the story, find the solution—whatever that is. Without it, your story won't connect.

Question #3: What Are the Barriers?

There are barriers between the conflict and the solution. These barriers are the things that so often hold us back from reaching the solution to the conflict. Those barriers might be things like fear, anxiety, hopelessness, or doubt.

When you speak to the barriers in the story, you have the opportunity to create a "that's me" moment with your viewer, because you can speak to the very barriers your audience faces in their own lives.

Question #4: What Is the Call to Action?

Sometimes we need another character, a guide, or an external force for us to overcome those barriers and seek the solution.

When you find the call to action in the story, you identify the thing that compelled someone to change and overcome the barriers they face.

It's critical for us as the church to zero in on this because the answer to what compelled someone to change is often the same next step others need to take in their own lives.

———

I found that as I focused on identifying the clear conflict, solution, barriers, and call to action in the story, the impact and reach of the stories we were telling became greater than ever before.

By answering those questions, you have the building blocks for telling meaningful stories that can inspire your audience.

We're all storytellers. What story will you tell?

Discuss

- What's your favorite story? Why?
  - What was the conflict?
  - What was the solution?
  - What barriers had to be overcome?
  - What was the call to action?
- What are some stories your church needs to share?

REACHING YOUNGER GENERATIONS

Churches have long had a challenge reaching the younger generation. Twenty-somethings, millennials, young adults—whatever buzzword you want to use to describe them. Attendance and engagement is in decline, so churches panic and look for an answer.

Is it a new program or service?
Is it adding some cool moving lights or starting new social media accounts?
Maybe it's just copying what the biggest church in town is doing?

In an effort to reach young people, many churches violate the foundation that will make them effective: authenticity.

Here's the superpower the younger generations are born with: they can sniff out authenticity. They know when you're just trying to sell something to them, get something from them, or be something you aren't. This superpower is what draws them to certain organizations or people and what turns them away from others.

What Does This Mean for the Church?

If we're going to effectively reach young people, we have to move beyond gimmicks and tactics. It means we have to take a hard look at the very heart behind the unique calling God has placed on us as leaders and churches.

Where Are Churches and Leaders Going Wrong?

Chasing "Cool"

There's nothing inherently wrong with cool lights, louder music, marketing campaigns, or any other methods churches can use. The problem is when churches try to add gimmicks and methods in an attempt to attract a younger audience when those methods don't fit who they authentically are. You can't just copy something that's working in another culture or church and assume it's going to work the same way for your unique culture.

Seeking the Perception of Perfection

Everybody knows no one is perfect. So why do we spend so much time trying to give the perception that we are? While we may seek the respect and adoration of our audience through giving off this perception of perfection, we actually miss out on real opportunities to connect and relate to them.

This is even a challenge pastors and church leaders face. The reality is young people (and I would argue, all people) are more drawn to your imperfections and scars than your perceived perfection, because it makes you relatable.

Trying to Be Something They're Not

Is there a disconnect between what your website says you are and what you actually are? Are you communicating to your guests that you are a young/hip/diverse church, only to have them arrive and find something completely different?

Young people want you to be you. If you're not what you want to be, pray bold prayers and make bold changes to become who God is calling you to be.

Trying to Make it Just a Program

It's far easier to start a new program for young people than it is to make bold changes as a whole church to reach the next generation. Many churches try to outsource their outreach for the younger generations through some add-on program or service and keep everything else the same. There's nothing wrong with targeting a certain demographic with a program or event, but this approach can trick you into believing you've solved the problem. The reality is you may have only delayed the inevitable of making hard decisions and changes that will make you more effective for reaching the next generation and beyond.

247

———

Trends and information about the younger generations are constantly changing. The next generation itself is always in flux. What works this year may not work five years from now.

Here's the bottomline: If you want to reach young people, you can't just read a research report on millennials and slap a picture of younger people on your website. You can't just put your pastor in skinny jeans and expect connection to magically happen. You can't just play new music and expect new people to show up.

You have to form an authentic connection.

So if you're not content with how your church is reaching young people, it might be time to figure out why. Do the hard work. Then, and only then, can you begin to wrestle with changes you may need to make.

Young people in your community are searching for something from your church.

It's not excellence.
It's not coolness.
It's not perfection.
It's authenticity.

Embrace the calling we all have in ministry of being a church full of imperfect people, chasing after a perfect God. Authenticity always wins.

Discuss

- For your church, take a moment to evaluate your efforts in reaching younger generations:

  - What is working?

  - Not working?

  - Missing?

  - Confusing?

- What might you need to start doing—or stop doing—to communicate more authentically as a church?

- How can you lead with more authenticity in your own personal leadership and ministry?

HEALTHY AND SUSTAINABLE

———

Over the last 10 years of working in the church, there's one word that comes up in almost every conversation I have with church leaders. That word is busy.

Busy with all that's happening in the church.
Busy with family.
Busy trying to react to all that life is throwing at them.

Busy isn't bad, until busy leads to an unhealthy and unsustainable pace.

What's your status today as a leader? Are you at a healthy and sustainable pace? Or are you on your way to burnout?

As you think about your status today, take a moment and work through these questions.

Status Check Questions

❏ **Question #1: What are your time suckers?**

As you look back at your calendar and think about how your time is spent, what are the things that take up a bunch of time but maybe aren't adding much value to your church or your leadership? These could be tasks, meetings, unhealthy rhythms, or areas of leadership that are becoming time suckers and pulling you off mission.

❏ **Question #2: What do you wish you had time for?**

If someone gave you an additional 10 hours this week, how would you invest that time? Would you create sustainable systems? Would you take more time investing in and developing volunteers? Where are the areas that you are discontent and want to be able to accomplish more?

❏ **Question #3: Who are you investing in?**

Who are the people on your team, whether that's staff or volunteers, that you are developing and investing into? This might even be someone who could someday replace you. As I've talked with other creatives, this is one of the most overlooked areas. But it's one of the most important things we can be doing as leaders. So who are you investing in right now?

OK, this next question may sting a little.

❏ **Question #4: When is your sabbath day?**

What day are you intentionally turning off your computer, turning off your phone notifications, and taking your sabbath day? Rest is essential to healthy and sustainable leadership. If you're working in the church, your sabbath day may not be on a Sunday. But that doesn't make it any less important for you to have a day blocked off on your calendar to intentionally shut down and recharge for the week ahead of you.

❏ **Question #5: Is your current pace sustainable?**

Think about the pace you're going at right now. If nothing changed in the next six months with your workload or the hours you're putting in—would you be at a sustainable pace? Or would you be on the edge of burnout? What are the things keeping you stuck in survival mode?

Come to Terms With Busy

There's no doubt these are hard questions. But it's also a hard job. If you're not taking care of yourself, you're not going to be doing this job for long.

So take care of yourself.

Because, as my friend Kelley Hartnett says, "It's probably not going to get better after Easter." Or Christmas. Or fall kickoff. Or whatever major event your church has coming up.

It's always going to be busy, so you need to figure out how to be healthy and sustainable in the midst of the busy.

Tip: If you need more help with that, Kelley Hartnett wrote a book with chapters on avoiding burnout, asking for help, saying no, dealing with perfectionism, and more. Check out *You've Got This: A Pep Talk for Church Communicators* (grab a free sample at PepTalkBook.com)

Discuss

- What's your status today? Are you closer to a healthy and sustainable pace? Or are you closer to burnout?

- As you answer the questions from this section and consider creating a more healthy and sustainable pace...

  – What do you think you need to start?

  – What do you think you need to stop?

  – What do you think you need to continue doing?

A LAST WORD

Thank you so much for investing your time into this book. My hope and prayer is that this book helped you rethink communication in your church, and gave you a practical playbook to communicate your message.

Communication is hard work. It can be challenging and overwhelming at times, but it's worth every ounce of energy you put into it. I know all too well that the enemy loves to tell you your work doesn't matter, it's not worth it, and there's just too far to go. Don't listen. God can do abundantly more than you can ask or imagine, and he does it through you.

You have the greatest message in the world to communicate. A message your community desperately needs to hear. Don't give up! You can embrace the new reality and recognize the ministry of communication. You can follow the communication playbook and rethink and rework how you've always done things. You can revolutionize how your church communicates and actually connect with your community.

Here's what I want to leave you with: In everything you do, with everything you communicate, focus on one thing: Put Jesus on display.

Keep it simple. Put Jesus on display.

In John 12:32, Jesus says, "When I am lifted up from the earth, I will draw everyone to myself."

It's not your job to grow your church. That's not on you. God never placed that on your shoulders. What you can do is focus on being faithful to what God has called you to do, and trust that when you put Jesus on display, he will draw all people to himself.

As you focus on putting Jesus on display, know this: Jesus says in Matthew 16:18, "I will build my church, and the gates of hell shall not prevail against it."

Put Jesus on display with everything you do and everything you communicate. That will bridge the gap between the best you can do and what God can do.

Do the best you can with what you have.
Rethink the way your church has always done it.
Take care of yourself.

And above all else, put Jesus on display.

ENDNOTES

———

New Reality: Attendance

1. Barna Trends 2017.

2. Public Religion Research Institute, "Exodus: Why Americans Are Leaving Religion—and Why They're Unlikely to Come Back," https://www.prri.org/research/prri-rns-poll-nones-atheist-leaving-religion/, accessed Nov. 28, 2018.

New Reality: Engagement

3. Social Media Today, "How Much Time Do People Spend on Social Media?" https://www.socialmediatoday.com/marketing/how-much-time-do-people-spend-social-media-infographic, accessed Nov. 28, 2018.

New Reality: Attention

4. Source Global Research, "Attention Spans Are Getting Shorter. Or Are They?" https://www.sourceglobalresearch.com/blog/2018/02/15/attention-spans-are-getting-shorter-or-are-they, accessed Nov. 28, 2018.

5. American Marketing Association, "Why Your Customers' Attention Is the Scarcest Resource in 2017," https://www.ama.org/partners/content/Pages/why-customers-attention-scarcest-resources-2017.aspx, accessed Nov. 28, 2018.

Communication Playbook: Clarify Your Message: Barriers

6. Barna, "What Millennials Want When They Visit Church," https://www.barna.com/research/what-millennials-want-when-they-visit-church/, accessed Nov. 28, 2018.

Rethink and Rework: Social Media Playbook

7. Pew Research Center, "Social Media Use in 2018," http://www.pewinternet.org/2018/03/01/social-media-use-in-2018/, accessed Dec. 3, 2018.

FREE RESOURCES

———

Throughout this book Phil referenced a few resources he's created that you can download to help you rethink communication, including a message communication plan template and church-wide communication grid. Take your next step in rethinking communication by downloading these resources and more.

More: RethinkCommunicationBook.com/resources
(available for a limited time)

ABOUT THE AUTHOR

 Phil Bowdle got his start in church as a pastor's kid making faces at his dad while he preached. Growing up, he had no desire to go into ministry. Now there's nothing he'd rather do.

After starting in creative ministry in 2004, today Phil is the creative arts pastor at West Ridge Church in Northwest Atlanta. He leads a team of creatives in the areas of communication, media, worship, and production. He also speaks, offers communication and creative coaching, and blogs about communication, leadership, and the creative church.

How To Contact Phil

Cell: 678.653.2047 *(seriously, give him a call)*
Email: Phil@PhilBowdle.com
Online: PhilBowdle.com

Coaching & Consulting
Do you need help rethinking communication and creative ministry in your church? Phil can help. To connect with Phil about one-on-one coaching or on-site consulting, email him at Phil@PhilBowdle.com.

ABOUT THE CENTER FOR CHURCH COMMUNICATION

We are a firebrand of communicators, sparking churches to communicate the gospel clearly, effectively, and without compromise.

The Center for Church Communication is a nonprofit organized by communication professionals who have been serving the church since 1998.

We help local churches communicate better.

As God's story comes alive to us and others, we see gospel-centered, local churches that captivate the attention and liberate the imagination of their community, resulting in more people saying, **"That's what church should be!"**

Check out two of our most helpful projects:

Church Marketing Sucks

Since 2004, we've frustrated, educated, and motivated church communicators to do a better job telling the greatest story ever told. With articles, resources, and challenging opinions, we further the conversation about what it means for churches to communicate well. **More:** ChurchMarketingSucks.com

Courageous Storytellers

Church communication is hard. Courageous Storytellers can help. We offer easily digestible and super-practical resources to help overwhelmed church communicators get it done. Every month we add fresh content focused on a specific theme, so our library of tips, tricks, and tools gets better all the time. **More:** CourageousStorytellers.com

MORE CHURCH COMMUNICATION HELP

Check out these other books from the Center for Church Communication to get more ideas and inspiration:

Unwelcome: 50 Ways Churches Drive Away First-Time Visitors
Jonathan Malm talks about ways churches can be unintentionally scaring guests away. He offers practical advice for how to be more welcoming and keep guests in the pews. These helpful tips will encourage pastors and communicators alike.
More: UnwelcomeBook.com

You've Got This: A Pep Talk for Church Communicators
We get it: Church communication can be a challenge. You feel overworked, overwhelmed, and overloaded. In her honest and self-deprecating style, Kelley Hartnett offers a pep talk that's part hug and part first-bump.
More: PepTalkBook.com

ACKNOWLEDGMENTS

—

Writing this book has been a dream of mine for many years, but it never would have become a reality without these people. So thank you:

To my wife and best friend, Sarah, who never wavered in her encouragement and support (even through all the late nights and early mornings working on this book).

To my parents, Bill and Janet Bowdle. I'm blessed beyond measure to have you as parents. Your love and service to the church has changed countless lives, including mine.

To my pastor, Brian Bloye, for your vision to plant West Ridge Church and for always pointing people to Jesus. Thank you for modeling courageous leadership, and for always being willing to rethink how we do what we do to reach those far from God.

To the leadership team at West Ridge Church, thank you for your friendship and support. I never dreamed of being able to serve with such incredible people.

To my creative dream team at West Ridge Church. Thanks for pouring all you have into putting Jesus on display. I'm grateful for every moment, every meeting, every cup of coffee, and every *Friends* or *The Office* quote we share together.

To friends who have supported and inspired me, I'm grateful for Stephen Brewster, Kem Meyer, Tony Morgan, Justin Dean, Van Baird, Paul Richardson, Steve Veale, Brian Kase, Mac Lake, Brady Shearer, Dave Adamson, Lori Bailey, Kelley Hartnett, Jonathan Malm, and many others.

To Joe Cavazos for your amazing work on the cover design.

To the Center for Church Communication team for making this book happen. Thank you Brad Abare for your vision to equip and encourage church communicators. Thank you Chuck Scoggins for seeing potential in this book and getting it off the ground. Thank you Mark MacDonald for your friendship and guidance in making this book a reality. Thank you Kevin D. Hendricks for editing and making this book one hundred times better than it ever would have been without you.

Most of all, all thanks and glory goes to Jesus Christ. Thank you Jesus for still using jacked up people like me to play a part in your story.

Made in the USA
Columbia, SC
10 June 2021